THE
COCKTAIL BIBLE

THE
COCKTAIL BIBLE

TRADITIONAL AND MODERN COCKTAILS FOR EVERY OCCASION

Linda Doeser

Photography by Chris Linton

p

This is a Parragon Publishing Book

This edition published in 2005

Parragon Publishing

Queen Street House

4 Queen Street

Bath BA1 1HE, UK

Created and produced for Parragon by The Bridgewater Book Company Ltd.

Cover Design Philip McIvor

Photography Chris Linton

Illustrations Ian Mitchell

Studio Manager Chris Morris

Mac Artwork Loraine Hayes

ISBN: 1-40545-915-8

Printed in China

NOTE

Recipes using uncooked eggs should be avoided by infants, the elderly, pregnant women,

convalescents, and anyone suffering from an illness.

Contents

Introduction 6

Classic Cocktails 12

Contemporary Cocktails 114

Non-alcoholic Cocktails 216

Glossary 254

Cocktail List 256

Introduction

Precisely where the word "cocktail" came from is uncertain. A popular piece of folklore describes how a Mexican princess named Xoctl offered a mixed drink to an American visitor to her father's court who confused her name with that of the drink itself. Another suggestion is that the spoon used for mixing drinks reminded imbibing racegoers of the docked tails of nonthoroughbred horses, called cocktails. There are many other flights of fancy, but modern etymologists mostly agree that the word derives from *coquetel*, a French, wine-based drink.

Whatever the origins of the word cocktail, mixed drinks have existed since ancient times, and the first recognizable cocktail dates from about the sixteenth century. Indeed, many classics have been around for much longer than most people think. The bourbon-based Old Fashioned, for example, first appeared at the end of the

eighteenth century. We know that the word cocktail was already in use in 1809 in the United States and, thirty-five years later, when the British novelist Charles Dickens described Major Pawkins as able to drink "more rum-toddy, mint-julep, gin-sling, and cock-tail, than any private gentleman of his acquaintance," it had reached Britain, too. Popular among the style-conscious and wealthy in the United States, cocktails were served before dinner in the most exclusive houses and hotels until World War I made them go out of fashion. They have gone in and out of vogue ever since.

Following the war, young people, disillusioned by the older generation and desperately seeking new experiences, pleasures, stimuli, and styles, developed a taste for a new range of cocktails. Ironically, Prohibition in the 1920s spurred on their development. Illegally produced liquor frequently tasted poisonous—and sometimes was—so its flavor needed to be

disguised with fruit juices and mixers. No doubt, the naughtiness of drinking alcoholic cocktails also added to their appeal to the "bright young things" of the time. The craze quickly crossed the Atlantic, and the best hotels in London,

Paris, and Monte Carlo, where the quality of gin and whiskey was more consistent, soon boasted their own cocktail bars.

World War II brought an end to such revelry and, although drunk occasionally, cocktails remained out of style for decades until an exuberant renaissance in the 1970s. This resulted in another new generation of recipes, often featuring white rum and vodka, and tequila, which was just becoming known outside its native Mexico. Inevitably, the pendulum swung against cocktails again until recently. Now, once more, the cocktail shaker is essential equipment in every fashionable city bar.

Essentials

Making, serving—and, above all, drinking—cocktails should be fun. All you need is some basic equipment, a few ingredients, and a sense of adventure.

Equipment

Classic cocktails are either shaken or stirred. A shaker is an essential piece of equipment, consisting of a container with an inner, perforated lid and an outer lid. Both lids are secured while the mixture is shaken, together with cracked ice, and then the cocktail is strained through the perforated lid into a glass.

A mixing glass is a medium-size pitcher in which stirred cocktails can be mixed. It is usually made of uncolored glass so you can see what you are doing.

A long-handled bar spoon is perfect for stirring and a small strainer prevents the ice cubes—used during mixing—from finding their way into the cocktail glass. Some modern cocktails, including slushes, are made in a blender or food processor, so if you have one, by all means make use of it. Any cocktail that is made by shaking can also be made in a blender.

Measuring cups, sometimes called "jiggers," and spoons are essential for getting the proportions right—guessing does not work. A corkscrew, bottle-opener, and sharp knife are crucial.

Other useful, but nonessential tools include a citrus reamer, an ice bucket and tongs, a punch bowl, a glass serving pitcher, and a zester or grater. If you have a juicer, this is useful for making large quantities of fresh juice for cocktails, and for preparing a hangover cure the morning after!

Glasses

You can serve cocktails in any glasses you like. Small, V-shaped, stemmed glasses may be worth buying, but it is not essential to have a full range of Old-fashioned, Highball, Collins glasses and so on. Medium and small straight-sided glasses and wine glasses cover most contingencies. Since part of their appeal is visual, cocktails are best served in clear, uncut glass. Chill the glasses in the refrigerator to ensure cocktails are cold.

Ingredients

You can stock your bar over a period of time with the basics—it is not necessary to buy everything at once. A good selection of alcoholic drinks would include whiskey, possibly Scotch and bourbon, brandy, gin, light and dark rum, triple sec, sweet and dry vermouth, vodka, and tequila. You could also include Pernod, beer, and red and white wine. Keep champagne cocktails for special occasions. Select your stock according to your tastes—for example, if you never drink whiskey, it would be extravagant to buy Scotch, Irish, Canadian, American blended, and bourbon.

Standard mixers include club soda, sparkling mineral water, cola, ginger ale, and tonic water. Freshly squeezed fruit juice is best, but when buying juice in a bottle or carton, avoid any with added sugar or extra "padding." Cranberry juice, for example, may be bulked with grape juice. Commercial brands of grapefruit, orange, cranberry, tomato juice, and lime cordial are useful.

A good supply of fresh lemons, limes, and oranges is essential. Fresh fruit is best, but if you use canned, buy it in natural juice rather than syrup, and drain well. Other useful garnishes and condiments include angostura bitters, Worcestershire sauce, and cocktail cherries. Finally, you can never have too much ice.

Techniques

Cracking and Crushing Ice

Store ice in the freezer until just before use. Cracked ice is used in both shaken and stirred cocktails. To crack ice, put ice cubes into a strong plastic bag and hit it against an outside wall, or put the ice between clean cloths on a sturdy counter and crush with a wooden mallet or rolling pin. Crushed ice is used in cocktails made in a blender. To crush ice, crack it as before but break it into much smaller pieces.

Frosting Glasses

Glasses can be frosted with sugar—or fine or coarse salt in the case of the Margarita or Salty Dog. Simply rub the rim of the glass with a wedge of lemon or lime, then dip the rim into a saucer of superfine sugar or fine salt until it is evenly coated.

Making Sugar Syrup

To make sugar syrup, put 4 tablespoons water and 4 tablespoons superfine sugar into a small pan and stir over low heat until the sugar has dissolved. Bring to a boil, then continue to boil, without stirring, for 1–2 minutes. Let cool, then refrigerate in a covered container for up to 2 weeks.

Shaken or Stirred?

To make a shaken cocktail, put fresh cracked ice into a cocktail shaker and pour over the other ingredients immediately. Secure the lids and shake vigorously for 10–20 seconds, until the outside of the shaker is coated in condensation. Strain into a glass and serve at once. To make a stirred cocktail, again use fresh cracked ice and pour over the ingredients immediately. Using a long-handled spoon, stir vigorously, without splashing, for 20 seconds, then strain into a glass and serve at once.

Classic Cocktails

Classic Cocktail

It cannot lay claim to being the first or even the only classic, but it has all the characteristic hallmarks of sophistication associated with cocktails.

serves 1

wedge of lemon

1 tsp superfine sugar

4–6 cracked ice cubes

2 measures brandy

½ measure clear Curaçao

½ measure Maraschino

½ measure lemon juice

lemon peel twist, to decorate

❶ Rub the rim of a chilled cocktail glass with the lemon wedge and then dip in the sugar to frost.

❷ Put the cracked ice into a cocktail shaker. Pour the brandy, Curaçao, Maraschino, and lemon juice over the ice and shake vigorously until a frost forms.

❸ Strain into the frosted glass and decorate with the lemon twist.

Variations

A number of cocktails are the quintessential classics of their type and named simply after the main ingredient.

Champagne Cocktail: place a sugar cube in the bottom of a chilled champagne flute and dash with Angostura bitters to douse it. Fill the glass with chilled champagne and decorate with a twist of lemon.

Tequila Cocktail: put 4–6 cracked ice cubes into a cocktail shaker. Dash Angostura bitters over the ice and pour in 3 measures golden tequila, 1 measure lime juice, and ½ measure grenadine. Shake vigorously until a frost forms, then strain into a chilled cocktail glass.

Brandy Cocktail: put 4–6 cracked ice cubes into a cocktail shaker. Dash Angostura bitters over the ice and pour in 2 measures brandy and ½ teaspoon sugar syrup (see page 11). Shake vigorously until a frost forms, then strain into a chilled cocktail glass and decorate with a twist of lemon.

Bartender's Tip

Maraschino is a sweet Italian liqueur made from cherries. It is usually white, but may also be colored red. The white version is better for most cocktails, because it does not affect the appearance of the finished drink.

Sangaree

Like Sangria, the name of this cocktail is derived from the Spanish word for blood and it was originally made with wine. Nowadays, it is more usually made with a spirit base, but whatever is used, it is invariably flavored with nutmeg.

serves 1

6 cracked ice cubes

2 measures brandy

1 measure sugar syrup (see page 11)

club soda, to top off

1 tsp port

pinch of freshly grated nutmeg

❶ Put the ice cubes into a chilled highball glass. Pour the brandy and sugar syrup over the ice and top off with club soda. Stir gently to mix.

❷ Float the port on top by pouring it gently over the back of a teaspoon and sprinkle with nutmeg.

Variations

Savoy Sangarees: for the first version, put 6 cracked ice cubes into a mixing glass. Pour 1 measure port over the ice, add 1 teaspoon superfine sugar, and stir until the sugar has dissolved. Strain into a chilled cocktail glass and sprinkle with freshly grated nutmeg. For the second version, substitute 1 measure sherry for the port.

Gin Sangaree: put 6 cracked ice cubes into a chilled glass. Pour 2 measures gin and ½ teaspoon sugar syrup (see page 11) over the ice and top off with sparkling mineral water. Stir gently to mix, then float 1 tablespoon port on top. Sprinkle with freshly grated nutmeg.

Scotch Sangaree: put 1 teaspoon clear honey in a chilled glass and add a little sparkling mineral water. Stir until the honey has dissolved. Add 6 cracked ice cubes. Pour 2 measures Scotch whisky over the ice and top off with sparkling water. Stir gently to mix, then decorate with a lemon twist, and sprinkle with freshly grated nutmeg.

Whiskey Sangaree: put 6 cracked ice cubes into a chilled glass. Pour 2 measures bourbon and 1 teaspoon sugar syrup (see page 11) over the ice and then top off with club soda. Stir gently to mix, then float 1 tablespoon ruby port on top. Sprinkle freshly grated nutmeg over the top.

Irish Canadian Sangaree: put 6 cracked ice cubes into a chilled glass. Pour 2 measures Canadian rye whisky, 1 measure Irish Mist, 1 measure lemon juice, and 1 measure orange juice over the ice, and stir gently. Sprinkle with freshly grated nutmeg.

Sidecar

Cointreau is the best-known brand of the orange-flavored liqueur known generically as triple sec. It is drier and stronger than Curaçao and is always colorless.

serves 1

4–6 cracked ice cubes
2 measures brandy
1 measure triple sec
1 measure lemon juice
orange peel twist, to decorate

❶ Put the ice into a cocktail shaker. Pour the brandy, triple sec, and lemon juice over the ice and shake vigorously until a frost forms.
❷ Strain into a chilled glass and decorate with the orange peel twist.

Variations

Champagne Sidecar: make a Sidecar as above, but strain it into a chilled champagne flute, and then top off with chilled champagne.

Chelsea Sidecar: put 4–6 cracked ice cubes into a cocktail shaker. Pour 2 measures gin, 1 measure triple sec, and 1 measure lemon juice over the ice. Shake vigorously until a frost forms, then strain into a chilled cocktail glass. Decorate with a lemon peel twist.

Boston Sidecar: put 4–6 cracked ice cubes into a cocktail shaker. Pour 1½ measures white rum, ½ measure brandy, ½ measure triple sec, and ½ measure lemon juice over the ice and shake vigorously until a frost forms. Strain into a chilled cocktail glass and decorate with an orange peel twist.

Polish Sidecar: put 4–6 cracked ice cubes into a cocktail shaker. Pour 2 measures gin, 1 measure blackberry brandy, and 1 measure lemon juice over the ice. Shake until a frost forms, then strain into a chilled cocktail glass. Decorate with a fresh blackberry.

Did you know?

You can buy "ice cubes" made from soapstone. Place them in the freezer to chill and use as you would ice cubes. They will not dilute your cocktails and will last forever.

B and B

Although elaborate concoctions are great fun to mix—and drink—some of the best cocktails are the simplest. B & B—brandy and Bénédictine—couldn't be easier, but it has a superbly subtle flavor.

serves 1

4–6 cracked ice cubes
1 measure brandy
1 measure Bénédictine

❶ Put the ice cubes into a mixing glass. Pour the brandy and Bénédictine over the ice and stir to mix.

❷ Strain into a chilled cocktail glass.

Variations

B and B Plus: add ½ measure lemon juice to the mixing glass when making a B & B.

Benedict: put 4–6 cracked ice cubes into a mixing glass. Pour 1 measure Bénédictine and 3 measures Scotch whisky over the ice. Stir gently to mix and strain into a chilled glass. Top off with dry ginger ale.

Big Boy: put 4–6 cracked ice cubes into a mixing glass. Pour 2 measures brandy, 1 measure triple sec, and 1 measure lemon juice over the ice. Stir to mix, then strain into a chilled cocktail glass.

Booster: put 4–6 cracked ice cubes into a cocktail shaker. Pour 2 measures brandy and 1 teaspoon clear Curaçao over the ice and add 1 egg white. Shake until a frost forms. Strain into a chilled cocktail glass.

French Connection: put 4–6 cracked ice cubes into a small, chilled glass. Pour 2 measures brandy and 1 measure amaretto over the ice. Stir well to mix. Half fill a small, chilled glass with cracked ice cubes and strain the cocktail over them.

Lugger: put 4–6 cracked ice cubes into a cocktail shaker. Pour 2 measures brandy, 1½ measures apple brandy, and ¼ teaspoon apricot brandy over the ice. Shake vigorously until a frost forms, then strain into a chilled cocktail glass.

Hell: put 4–6 cracked ice cubes into a mixing glass and add 1 measure brandy and 1 measure crème de menthe. Stir well to mix, then strain into a chilled cocktail glass. Sprinkle with a pinch of cayenne pepper.

Bartender's Tip

Bénédictine has been produced in a Normandy monastery since 1510. The recipe for this liqueur includes at least 17 herbs and natural flavorings, among them angelica, cilantro, thyme, hyssop, cloves, cinnamon, saffron, and honey—but the proportions are kept a closely guarded secret. There is no substitute for this liqueur.

Corpse Reviver

This cocktail is not designed to deal with a hangover the morning after, but is a great pick-me-up after a busy day to get you in the mood to party. Note that it will not prevent your needing a different kind of corpse reviver or some other sort of pick-me-up (see below) next day. None of these cocktails comes with a medical guarantee.

serves 1

4–6 cracked ice cubes
2 measures brandy
1 measure apple brandy
1 measure sweet vermouth

❶ Put the cracked ice into a mixing glass. Pour the brandy, apple brandy, and vermouth over the ice. Stir gently to mix.
❷ Strain into a chilled cocktail glass.

Other desperate measures

Savoy Corpse Reviver: put 4–6 cracked ice cubes into a mixing glass and add 1 measure brandy, 1 measure Fernet Branca, and 1 measure white crème de menthe. Stir well. Strain into a chilled cocktail glass.

Stomach Reviver: put 4–6 cracked ice cubes into a glass. Dash Angostura bitters over the ice and pour in 2 measures brandy, and 1 measure Fernet Branca. Stir well, then strain into a chilled cocktail glass.

Prairie Oyster: put 4–6 cracked ice cubes into a cocktail shaker. Dash Tabasco sauce over the ice and pour in 2 measures brandy, ½ measure Worcestershire sauce, ½ measure red wine vinegar, and 1 teaspoon tomato catsup. Shake until a frost forms. Strain into a chilled glass, float an unbroken egg yolk on top, and sprinkle with cayenne pepper. Swallow the cocktail in a single swig without breaking the egg yolk. (For a nonalcoholic Open Prairie Oyster, see page 218.)

Harry's Pick-Me-Up: put 4–6 cracked ice cubes into a cocktail shaker. Pour 2 measures brandy, 1 measure lemon juice, and 1 teaspoon grenadine over the ice. Shake vigorously until a frost forms. Pour into a chilled champagne flute and top off with chilled champagne.

Bartender's Tip

Grenadine is a sweet, pink-colored syrup made from pomegranates and can be used to sweeten and color both alcoholic and nonalcoholic cocktails. It has a distinctive, but not strong, flavor, and if you don't like it, you can substitute sugar syrup (see page 11). Grenadine is also very sweet, so you may wish to add less if you find it too sweet.

Stinger

Aptly named, this is a refreshing, clean-tasting cocktail to tantalize the taste buds and make you sit up and take notice. However, bear in mind that it packs a punch and if you have too many, you are likely to keel over.

serves 1

4–6 cracked ice cubes
2 measures brandy
1 measure white crème de menthe

❶ Put the ice cubes into a cocktail shaker. Pour the brandy and crème de menthe over the ice. Shake vigorously until a frost forms.

❷ Strain into a small, chilled highball glass.

Variations

Amaretto Stinger: put 4–6 cracked ice cubes into a cocktail shaker. Pour 2 measures amaretto and 1 measure white crème de menthe over the ice. Shake vigorously until a frost forms, then strain into a chilled cocktail glass.

Chocolate Stinger: put 4–6 cracked ice cubes into a cocktail shaker. Pour 1 measure dark crème de cacao and 1 measure white crème de menthe over the ice. Shake vigorously until a frost forms. Strain into a chilled cocktail glass.

Irish Stinger: put 4–6 cracked ice cubes into a cocktail shaker. Pour 1 measure Bailey's Irish Cream and 1 measure white crème de menthe over the ice. Shake vigorously until a frost forms, then strain into a chilled shot glass.

Did you know?

Bailey's Irish Cream is the world's top-selling liqueur and accounts for one percent of the Irish Republic's export revenue.

Between the Sheets

Since the name of this cocktail always seems to imply romance and hints that the sheets in question are, at the very least, satin, make it for two people. Certainly, this delicious concoction is as smooth as silk.

serves 2

8–10 cracked ice cubes
4 measures brandy
3 measures white rum
1 measure clear Curaçao
1 measure lemon juice

❶ Put the cracked ice into a cocktail shaker. Pour the brandy, rum, Curaçao, and lemon juice over the ice. Shake vigorously until a frost forms.
❷ Strain into two chilled wine glasses or goblets.

More romantic moments

These variations all serve one person.

Between Sheets: put 4–6 cracked ice cubes into a cocktail shaker. Pour 1 measure brandy, 1 measure white rum, 1 measure triple sec, and 1 measure lemon juice over the ice. Shake vigorously until a frost forms, then strain into a chilled shot glass.

Grand Passion: put 4–6 cracked ice cubes into a cocktail shaker and add 2 measures gin, 1 measure dry vermouth, 1 measure passion fruit syrup, and ½ measure lemon juice. Shake until a frost forms. Strain into a chilled cocktail glass and decorate with an orange peel twist.

Night of Passion: put 4–6 cracked ice cubes into a cocktail shaker. Pour 2 measures gin, 1 measure triple sec, 2 measures peach juice, 2 measures passion fruit juice, and 1 tablespoon lemon juice over the ice. Shake vigorously until a frost forms, then strain into a small, chilled glass.

Bedtime Bouncer: put 4–6 cracked ice cubes into a cocktail shaker. Pour 2 measures brandy and 1 measure triple sec over the ice. Shake vigorously until a frost forms and strain into a chilled glass. Top off with bitter lemon and decorate with an orange peel twist.

American Rose

"A rose by any other name..."—this Oscar-winning cocktail has, rightly, inspired roses across the world. It is truly a thing of beauty and a joy forever.

serves 1

4-6 cracked ice cubes
1½ measures brandy
1 tsp grenadine
½ tsp Pernod
½ fresh peach, peeled and mashed
sparkling wine, to top off
fresh peach wedge, to decorate

❶ Put the cracked ice into a cocktail shaker. Pour the brandy, grenadine, and Pernod over the ice and add the peaches. Shake vigorously until a frost forms.
❷ Strain into a chilled wine goblet and top off with sparkling wine. Stir gently, then garnish with the peach wedge.

Variations

White Rose: put 4-6 cracked ice cubes into a cocktail shaker. Dash lemon juice over the ice and pour in 3 measures gin, 1 measure Maraschino, and 1 measure orange juice. Shake vigorously until a frost forms, then strain into a chilled cocktail glass.

Bermuda Rose: put 4-6 cracked ice cubes into a cocktail shaker. Pour 2 measures gin, 2 teaspoons apricot brandy, 1 tablespoon lime juice, and 2 teaspoons grenadine over the ice. Shake vigorously until a frost forms. Fill a chilled glass with crushed ice cubes. Strain the cocktail into the glass and top off with sparkling mineral water. Decorate with a lime slice.

Russian Rose: put 4-6 cracked ice cubes into a mixing glass. Dash orange bitters over the ice and pour in 3 measures strawberry-flavored vodka, ½ measure dry vermouth, and ½ measure grenadine. Stir gently to mix and strain into a chilled cocktail glass.

English Rose: put 4-6 cracked ice cubes into a cocktail shaker. Dash lemon juice over the ice and pour in 2 measures gin, 2 measures dry vermouth, and 1 measure apricot brandy. Shake vigorously until a frost forms, then strain into a chilled cocktail glass.

Jack Rose: put 4-6 cracked ice cubes into a cocktail shaker. Add 2 measures Calvados or applejack brandy, ½ measure lime juice, and 1 teaspoon grenadine. Shake vigorously until a frost forms, then strain into a chilled cocktail glass.

Bartender's Tip

For a French Rose, see page 110.

Mint Julep

A julep is simply a mixed drink sweetened with syrup and it dates back to ancient times. The Mint Julep was probably first made in the United States, and is the traditional drink of the Kentucky Derby.

serves 1

leaves of 1 fresh mint sprig

1 tbsp sugar syrup (see page 11)

6–8 crushed ice cubes

3 measures bourbon whiskey

fresh mint sprig, to decorate

❶ Put the mint leaves and sugar syrup into a small, chilled glass and mash with a teaspoon. Add the crushed ice to fill the glass, then add the bourbon.

❷ Decorate with the mint sprig.

Variations

Frozen Mint Julep: put 4–6 crushed ice cubes into a blender or food processor. Add 2 measures bourbon whiskey, 1 measure lemon juice, 1 measure sugar syrup (see page 11), and 6 fresh mint leaves. Process at low speed until slushy. Pour into a small, chilled glass and decorate with a fresh mint sprig.

Brandy Julep: fill a chilled glass with cracked ice. Add 2 measures brandy, 1 teaspoon sugar syrup (see page 11), and 4 fresh mint leaves. Stir well to mix and decorate with a fresh mint sprig and a slice of lemon. Serve with a straw.

Jocose Julep: put 4–6 crushed ice cubes into a blender. Pour in 3 measures bourbon whiskey, 1 measure green crème de menthe, 1½ measures lime juice, and 1 teaspoon sugar syrup (see page 11). Add 5 fresh mint leaves. Process until smooth. Fill a chilled glass with cracked ice cubes and pour in the cocktail. Top off with sparkling mineral water and stir gently. Decorate with a fresh mint sprig.

Bartender's Tip

For a nonalcoholic Juicy Julep, see page 230.

Did you know?

The word "julep" is derived from Persian and came to us via Arabic. It means rose-water.

Whiskey Sour

Sours are short drinks, flavored with lemon or lime juice. They can be made with almost any spirit, although Whiskey Sour was the original and, for many, is still the favorite.

serves 1

4–6 cracked ice cubes
2 measures American blended whiskey
1 measure lemon juice
1 tsp sugar syrup (see page 11)

To decorate
cocktail cherry
slice of orange

❶ Put the cracked ice into a cocktail shaker. Pour the whiskey, lemon juice, and sugar syrup over the ice. Shake vigorously until a frost forms.

❷ Strain into a chilled cocktail glass and decorate with the cherry and orange slice.

Variations

Bourbon Sour: substitute bourbon for the blended whiskey and decorate with a slice of orange.

Brandy Sour: substitute 2½ measures brandy for the blended whiskey.

Boston Sour: add 1 egg white to the ingredients in the cocktail shaker. Decorate with a cocktail cherry and a lemon slice.

Polynesian Sour: put 4–6 cracked ice cubes into a cocktail shaker and add 2 measures white rum, ½ measure lemon juice, ½ measure orange juice, and ½ measure guava juice. Shake until a frost forms, then pour into a chilled cocktail glass. Decorate with a slice of orange.

Fireman's Sour: put 4–6 cracked ice cubes into a cocktail shaker and add 2 measures white rum, 1½ measures lime juice, 1 tablespoon grenadine, and

1 teaspoon sugar syrup (see page 11). Shake until a frost forms. Strain into a cocktail glass and decorate with a cocktail cherry and a slice of lemon.

Strega Sour: put 4–6 cracked ice cubes into a cocktail shaker. Pour 2 measures gin, 1 measure Strega, and 1 measure lemon juice over the ice. Shake vigorously until a frost forms. Strain into a cocktail glass and decorate with a slice of lemon.

Double Standard Sour: put 4–6 cracked ice cubes into a cocktail shaker and add 1½ measures blended whiskey, 1½ measures gin, 1 measure lemon juice, 1 teaspoon grenadine, and 1 teaspoon sugar syrup (see page 11). Shake until a frost forms. Strain into a chilled cocktail glass and decorate with a cocktail cherry and a slice of orange.

Manhattan

Said to have been invented by Sir Winston Churchill's American mother, Jennie, the Manhattan is one of many cocktails named after places in New York City. The center of sophistication in the Jazz Age, the city is, once again, buzzing with cocktail bars for a new generation.

serves 1

4–6 cracked ice cubes
dash of Angostura bitters
3 measures rye whiskey
1 measure sweet vermouth
cocktail cherry, to decorate

❶ Put the cracked ice into a mixing glass. Dash the Angostura bitters over the ice and pour in the whiskey and vermouth. Stir well to mix.

❷ Strain into a chilled glass and decorate with the cherry.

City lights

Harlem Cocktail: put 4–6 cracked ice cubes into a cocktail shaker. Pour 2 measures gin, 1½ measures pineapple juice, and 1 teaspoon Maraschino over the ice, and add 1 tablespoon chopped fresh pineapple. Shake vigorously until a frost forms, then strain into a small, chilled glass.

Brooklyn: put 4–6 cracked ice cubes into a mixing glass. Dash Amer Picon and Maraschino over the ice and pour in 2 measures rye whiskey and 1 measure dry vermouth. Stir to mix, then strain into a chilled cocktail glass.

Broadway Smile: pour 1 measure chilled triple sec into a small, chilled glass. With a steady hand, pour 1 measure chilled crème de cassis on top, without

mixing, then carefully pour 1 measure chilled Swedish Punsch on top, again without mixing.

Fifth Avenue: pour 1½ measures chilled dark crème de cacao into a small, chilled, straight-sided glass. With a steady hand, pour 1½ measures chilled apricot brandy on top, without mixing, then carefully pour ¾ measure chilled light cream on top, again without mixing.

Coney Island Baby: put 4–6 cracked ice cubes into a cocktail shaker. Pour 2 measures peppermint schnapps and 1 measure dark crème de cacao over the ice. Shake vigorously until a frost forms. Fill a small, chilled glass with cracked ice and strain the cocktail over it. Top off with club soda and stir gently.

Old Fashioned

So ubiquitous is this cocktail that a small, straight-sided glass is known as an Old Fashioned glass. It is a perfect illustration of the saying, "Sometimes the old ones are the best."

serves 1

sugar cube

dash of Angostura bitters

1 tsp water

2 measures bourbon or rye whiskey

4–6 cracked ice cubes

lemon peel twist, to decorate

❶ Place the sugar cube in a small, chilled Old Fashioned glass. Dash the bitters over the cube and add the water. Mash with a spoon until the sugar has dissolved.

❷ Pour the bourbon or rye whiskey into the glass and stir. Add the cracked ice cubes and decorate with the lemon peel twist.

"Not old, but mellow"

Brandy Old Fashioned: place a sugar cube in a small, chilled glass. Dash Angostura bitters over the sugar to douse and add a dash of water. Mash with a spoon until the sugar has dissolved, then pour in 3 measures brandy and add 4–6 cracked ice cubes. Stir gently and decorate with a lemon peel twist.

Old Etonian: put 4–6 cracked ice cubes into a mixing glass. Dash crème de noyaux and orange bitters over the ice and pour in 1 measure gin and 1 measure Lillet. Stir, then strain into a chilled cocktail glass. Squeeze over a piece of orange peel.

Old Pal: put 4–6 cracked ice cubes into a cocktail shaker. Pour 2 measures rye whiskey, 1½ measures Campari, and

1 measure sweet vermouth over the ice. Shake vigorously until a frost forms, then strain into a chilled cocktail glass.

Old Trout: put 4–6 cracked ice cubes into a cocktail shaker. Pour 1 measure Campari and 2 measures orange juice over the ice. Shake vigorously until a frost forms. Fill a tall glass with ice cubes and strain the cocktail over them. Top off with sparkling mineral water and decorate with a slice of orange.

Old Pale: put 4–6 cracked ice cubes into a mixing glass. Pour 2 measures bourbon, 1 measure Campari, and 1 measure dry vermouth over the ice. Stir well, then strain into a chilled cocktail glass. Squeeze over a piece of lemon peel.

Boilermaker

Originally, boilermaker was slang for a shot of whiskey followed by a beer chaser. This version is marginally more sophisticated, but every bit as lethal.

serves 1

1 cup English Pale Ale
1½ measures bourbon or rye whiskey

❶ Pour the beer into a chilled beer glass or tankard. Pour the bourbon or rye whiskey into a chilled shot glass.
❷ Gently submerge the shot glass in the beer.

Variations

Depth Charge: pour 2 measures of schnapps—choose your favorite flavor—into a chilled beer glass or tankard, then pour in 2 cups English Pale Ale.

Submarino: pour 1 cup Mexican beer into a chilled beer glass or tankard. Pour 2 measures white tequila into a chilled shot glass, then gently submerge the shot glass in the beer.

Yorsh: pour 1 cup English Pale Ale into a chilled beer glass or tankard, then pour in 2 measures vodka.

Ginger Beer: pour 1 cup dark beer into a chilled beer glass or tankard, then pour in 2 measures ginger brandy.

Dog's Nose: pour 1 cup English Pale Ale into a chilled beer glass or tankard, then pour in 1 measure gin.

Bartender's Tip

You can use your favorite beer for making any of these drinks, although certain types are traditional for making particular cocktails.

Martini

For many, this is the ultimate cocktail. It is named after its inventor, Martini de Anna de Toggia, and not the famous brand of vermouth. The original version comprised equal measures of gin and vermouth, now known as a Fifty-Fifty, but the proportions vary, up to the Ultra Dry Martini, when the glass is merely rinsed out with vermouth before the gin is poured in.

serves 1

4–6 cracked ice cubes
3 measures gin
1 tsp dry vermouth, or to taste
cocktail olive, to decorate

❶ Put the cracked ice cubes into a mixing glass. Pour the gin and vermouth over the ice and stir well to mix.

❷ Strain into a chilled cocktail glass and decorate with a cocktail olive.

Variations

Gibson: decorate with 2–3 cocktail onions, instead of an olive.

Vodka Martini: substitute vodka for the gin.

Tequini: put 4–6 cracked ice cubes into a mixing glass. Dash Angostura bitters over the ice and pour in 3 measures white tequila and ½ measure dry vermouth. Stir well to mix, strain into a chilled cocktail glass and decorate with a twist of lemon.

Dirty Martini: put 4–6 cracked ice cubes into a cocktail shaker. Pour 3 measures gin, 1 measure dry vermouth, and ½ measure brine from a jar of cocktail olives over the ice. Shake vigorously until a frost forms. Strain into a chilled cocktail glass and decorate with a cocktail olive.

Bartender's Tip

For an Ultimate Beefeater Martini, see page 78. For a Hot and Dirty Martini and a Fuzzy Martini, see page 176. For a Sapphire Martini and a Topaz Martini, see page 210. For a Cool Yule Martini, see page 214.

Did you know?

Not only did James Bond always demand that his Martini should be shaken, not stirred, but his creator, Ian Fleming, also followed this practice.

Bronx

Like Manhattan, the New York borough of the Bronx—and also the river
of the same name—have been immortalized in cocktail bars throughout
the world.

serves 1

4–6 cracked ice cubes
2 measures gin
1 measure orange juice
½ measure dry vermouth
½ measure sweet vermouth

❶ Put the cracked ice cubes into a mixing
glass. Pour the gin, orange juice, and dry
and sweet vermouth over the ice. Stir
to mix.
❷ Strain into a chilled cocktail glass.

Variations

Bronx River: put 4–6 cracked ice cubes
into a cocktail shaker. Pour 2 measures
gin, 1 measure sweet vermouth, 1 measure
lemon juice, and ½ teaspoon sugar syrup
(see page 11) over the ice. Shake vigorously
until a frost forms. Strain into a chilled
cocktail glass.

Bronx Silver: put 4–6 cracked ice cubes
into a cocktail shaker. Pour 2 measures
gin, 1 measure orange juice, ½ measure
dry vermouth, and 1 egg white over the
ice. Shake vigorously until a frost forms,
then strain into a chilled cocktail glass.

Bronx Cheer: almost fill a tall glass
with cracked ice cubes. Pour 2 measures
apricot brandy over the ice and top off
with raspberry soda. Stir gently, decorate

with orange peel and a fresh raspberry,
and serve with a straw.

Bronx Empress: put 4–6 cracked ice
cubes into a cocktail shaker. Dash Pernod
over the ice and pour in 1 measure gin,
1 measure orange juice, and 1 measure
dry vermouth. Shake vigorously until
a frost forms. Strain into a chilled
cocktail glass.

Bronx Terrace: put 4–6 cracked ice cubes
into a cocktail shaker. Pour 2 measures
gin, 1 measure lime juice, and ½ measure
dry vermouth over the ice. Shake
vigorously until a frost forms. Strain
into a chilled cocktail glass and decorate
with a cocktail cherry.

White Lady

Simple, elegant, subtle, and much more powerful than appearance suggests, this is the perfect cocktail to serve before an *al fresco* summer dinner.

serves 1

4–6 cracked ice cubes
2 measures gin
1 measure triple sec
1 measure lemon juice

❶ Put the ice into a cocktail shaker. Pour the gin, triple sec, and lemon juice over the ice. Shake vigorously until a frost forms.
❷ Strain into a chilled cocktail glass.

Variations

Green Lady: put 4–6 cracked ice cubes into a cocktail shaker. Dash lime juice over the ice and pour in 2 measures gin and 1 measure green Chartreuse. Shake vigorously until a frost forms, then strain into a chilled cocktail glass.

Creole Lady: put 4–6 cracked ice cubes into a mixing glass. Pour 2 measures bourbon, 1½ measures Madeira, and 1 teaspoon grenadine over the ice. Stir well to mix, then strain into a chilled cocktail glass. Decorate with cocktail cherries.

Perfect Lady: put 4–6 cracked ice cubes into a cocktail shaker. Pour 2 measures gin, 1 measure peach brandy, and 1 measure lemon juice over the ice. Add 1 teaspoon egg white. Shake until a frost forms. Strain into a chilled cocktail glass.

Apricot Lady: put 4–6 cracked ice cubes into a cocktail shaker. Pour 1½ measures white rum, 1 measure apricot brandy, 1 tablespoon lime juice, and ½ teaspoon triple sec over the ice, and add 1 egg white.

Shake vigorously until a frost forms. Half fill a small, chilled glass with cracked ice. Strain the cocktail over the ice and decorate with a slice of orange.

Blue Lady: put 4–6 cracked ice cubes into a cocktail shaker. Pour 2½ measures blue Curaçao, 1 measure white crème de cacao, and 1 measure light cream over the ice. Shake until a frost forms, then strain into a chilled cocktail glass.

My Fair Lady: put 4–6 cracked ice cubes into a cocktail shaker. Dash strawberry liqueur over the ice, pour in 2 measures gin, 1 measure orange juice, 1 measure lemon juice, and add 1 egg white. Shake vigorously until a frost forms. Strain into a chilled cocktail glass.

Shady Lady: put 4–6 cracked ice cubes into a cocktail shaker. Dash lime juice over the ice and pour in 3 measures tequila, 1 measure apple brandy, and 1 measure cranberry juice. Shake until a frost forms. Strain into a chilled cocktail glass.

Alexander

This creamy, chocolate-flavored, gin-based cocktail, decorated with grated nutmeg, is the head of an extended family of cocktails, which continues to grow.

serves 1

4–6 cracked ice cubes
1 measure gin
1 measure crème de cacao
1 measure light cream
freshly grated nutmeg, to decorate

❶ Put the cracked ice cubes into a cocktail shaker. Pour the gin, crème de cacao, and light cream over the ice. Shake vigorously until a frost forms.

❷ Strain into a chilled cocktail glass and sprinkle with the nutmeg.

Family connections

Alexander's Sister: put 4–6 cracked ice cubes into a cocktail shaker. Pour 2 measures gin, 1 measure green crème de menthe, and 1 measure light cream over the ice. Shake until a frost forms, then strain into a chilled cocktail glass and decorate with freshly grated nutmeg.

Alexander's Sister-in-law: put 4–6 cracked ice cubes into a cocktail shaker. Pour 1 measure gin, 1 measure white crème de menthe, and 1 measure light cream over the ice. Shake until a frost forms, strain into a chilled cocktail glass, and decorate with freshly grated nutmeg.

Alexander Baby: put 4–6 cracked ice cubes into a cocktail shaker. Pour 2 measures white rum, 1 measure crème de cacao, and ½ measure light cream over the ice. Shake until a frost forms, then strain into a chilled cocktail glass, and decorate with freshly grated nutmeg.

Brandy Alexander: put 4–6 cracked ice cubes into a cocktail shaker. Pour 1½ measures brandy, 1½ measures dark crème de cacao, and 1½ measures light cream over the ice. Shake vigorously until a frost forms, then strain into a chilled cocktail glass.

Bartender's Tip

For Alexander's Daughter, a nonalcoholic version, see page 246.

Tom Collins

This cocktail combines gin, lemon juice, and club soda to make a cooling long drink. This is a venerable cocktail, but the progenitor of several generations of the Collins family of drinks, scattered across the globe, was the popular John Collins cocktail.

serves 1

5–6 cracked ice cubes
3 measures gin
2 measures lemon juice
½ measure sugar syrup (see page 11)
club soda, to top off
slice of lemon, to decorate

❶ Put the cracked ice into a cocktail shaker. Pour the gin, lemon juice, and sugar syrup over the ice. Shake vigorously until a frost forms.
❷ Strain into a tall, chilled glass and top off with club soda. Decorate with a slice of lemon.

Variations

John Collins: substitute Dutch gin or genever for the dry gin.

Mick Collins: substitute Irish whiskey for the gin.

Pierre Collins: substitute brandy for the gin.

Pedro Collins: substitute white rum for the gin.

Colonel Collins: substitute bourbon for the gin.

Mac Collins: substitute Scotch whisky for the gin.

Ivan Collins: substitute vodka for the gin and decorate with a slice of orange and a cocktail cherry.

Belle Collins: crush 2 fresh mint sprigs and place in a tall, chilled glass. Add 4–6 crushed ice cubes and pour in 2 measures gin, 1 measure lemon juice, and 1 teaspoon sugar syrup (see page 11).

Top off with sparkling water, stir gently, and decorate with a fresh mint sprig.

Juan Collins: half fill a chilled glass with cracked ice cubes and pour in 2 measures white tequila, 1 measure lemon juice, and 1 teaspoon sugar syrup (see page 11). Top off with sparkling water and stir gently. Decorate with a cocktail cherry.

Country Cousin Collins: put 4–6 crushed ice cubes into a blender. Dash orange bitters over the ice. Add 2 measures apple brandy, 1 measure lemon juice, and ½ teaspoon sugar syrup (see page 11). Blend at medium speed for 10 seconds. Pour into a tall, chilled glass. Top off with sparkling water. Stir and decorate with a lemon slice.

Bartender's Tip

For a Cool Collins, a nonalcoholic version, see page 230.

Daisy

A Daisy is a long cocktail with a high proportion of alcohol and sweetened with fruit syrup. Perhaps it gets its name from the now old-fashioned slang when the word "daisy" referred to something exceptional and special.

serves 1

4–6 cracked ice cubes

3 measures gin

1 measure lemon juice

1 tbsp grenadine

1 tsp sugar syrup (see page 11)

club soda, to top off

slice of orange, to decorate

❶ Put the cracked ice cubes into a cocktail shaker. Pour the gin, lemon juice, grenadine, and sugar syrup over the ice. Shake vigorously until a frost forms.

❷ Strain into a chilled highball glass and top off with club soda. Stir gently, then decorate with an orange slice.

Variations

Star Daisy: put 4–6 cracked ice cubes into a cocktail shaker. Pour 2 parts gin, 1½ parts apple brandy, 1½ parts lemon juice, 1 teaspoon sugar syrup (see page 11), and ½ teaspoon triple sec over the ice. Shake vigorously until a frost forms, then strain into a chilled glass and top off with club soda.

Chartreuse Daisy: put 4–6 cracked ice cubes into a cocktail shaker. Dash lemon juice over the ice and pour in 2 measures brandy and 1 measure green Chartreuse. Shake vigorously until a frost forms, then strain into a chilled glass. Top off with sparkling mineral water.

Did you know?

Club soda was originally a natural sparkling mineral water. It was eventually replaced by mass-produced artificially carbonated water, but is now being superseded by sparkling mineral water once again.

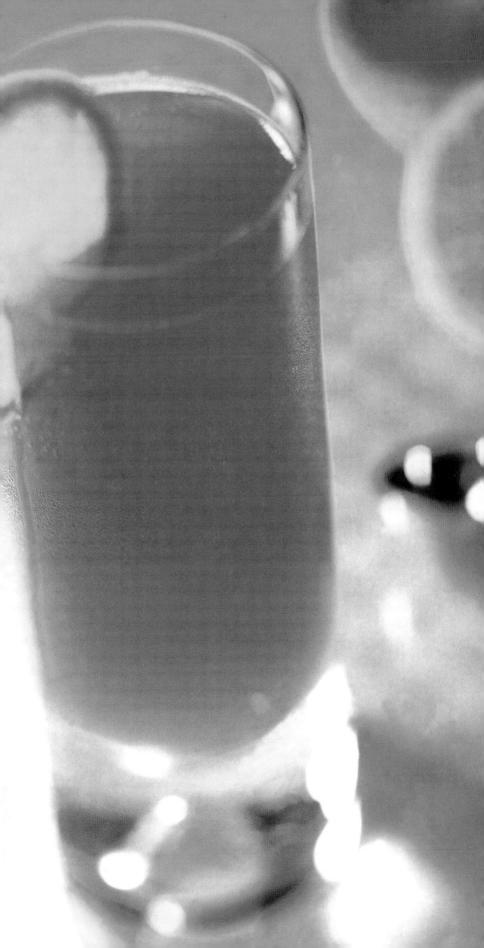

Orange Blossom

It is disappointing to discover that the pretty name of this cocktail is derived from the practice of adding fresh orange juice to bathtub gin during the years of Prohibition in order to conceal its filthy flavor. Made with good-quality gin, which needs no such concealment, it is delightfully refreshing.

serves 1

4–6 cracked ice cubes
2 measures gin
2 measures orange juice
slice of orange, to decorate

❶ Put the cracked ice cubes into a cocktail shaker. Pour the gin and orange juice over the ice and shake vigorously until a frost forms.

❷ Strain into a chilled cocktail glass and decorate with the orange slice.

Variations

Hawaiian Orange Blossom: put 4–6 cracked ice cubes into a cocktail shaker. Pour 2 measures gin, 1 measure triple sec, 2 measures orange juice, and 1 measure pineapple juice over the ice. Shake vigorously until a frost forms, then strain into a chilled wine glass.

Kentucky Orange Blossom: put 4–6 cracked ice cubes into a cocktail shaker. Pour 2 measures bourbon, 1 measure orange juice, and 1/2 measure triple sec over the ice. Shake vigorously until a frost forms. Strain into a chilled cocktail glass and decorate with a slice of orange.

Magnolia Blossom: put 4–6 cracked ice cubes into a cocktail shaker. Pour 2 measures gin, 1 measure lemon juice, and 1 measure light cream over the ice. Shake vigorously until a frost forms. Strain into a chilled cocktail glass.

Apple Blossom: put 4–6 cracked ice cubes into a mixing glass. Pour 2 measures brandy, 1 1/2 measures apple juice, and 1/2 teaspoon lemon juice over the ice, and stir well to mix. Half fill a small, chilled glass with ice and strain the cocktail over it. Decorate with a slice of lemon.

Cherry Blossom: put 4–6 cracked ice cubes into a cocktail shaker. Dash clear Curaçao, grenadine, and lemon juice over the ice, and pour in 2 measures brandy and 2 measures cherry brandy. Shake vigorously until a frost forms, then strain into a chilled cocktail glass.

Club

Groucho Marx is well known for claiming that he wouldn't want to belong to any club that was prepared to accept him as a member. This Club and its many associates are unlikely ever to have any shortage of willing members.

serves 1

4–6 cracked ice cubes
dash of yellow Chartreuse
2 measures gin
1 measure sweet vermouth

❶ Put the cracked ice cubes into a mixing glass. Dash the Chartreuse over the ice and pour in the gin and vermouth. Stir well to mix.

❷ Strain into a chilled cocktail glass.

Variations

Clover Club: put 4–6 cracked ice cubes into a cocktail shaker. Pour 2 measures gin, 1 measure lime juice, and 1 measure grenadine over the ice, and add 1 egg white. Shake vigorously until a frost forms, then strain into a chilled cocktail glass.

Grand Royal Clover Club: make a Clover Club and substitute lemon juice for the lime juice.

Racquet Club: put 4–6 cracked ice cubes into a mixing glass. Dash orange bitters over the ice and pour in 1 measure gin and 1 measure dry vermouth. Stir well to mix, then strain into a chilled cocktail glass.

Pegu Club: put 4–6 cracked ice cubes into a cocktail shaker. Dash lime juice, Angostura bitters, and orange bitters over the ice and pour in 1 measure gin, and 1 measure clear Curaçao. Shake vigorously until a frost forms, then strain into a chilled cocktail glass.

Key Club: put 4–6 cracked ice cubes into a cocktail shaker. Pour 2 measures gin, ½ measure dark rum, ½ measure Falernum, and ½ measure lime juice over the ice. Shake vigorously until a frost forms. Strain into a cocktail glass and decorate with pineapple wedges.

Bartender's Tip

Falernum is a Caribbean syrup made from fruit, sugar cane, and spices. It is used to sweeten both alcoholic and nonalcoholic cocktails. It is available from specialty Caribbean stores, but may be difficult to find in some places. There is no real substitute, but you could try using a mixture of sugar syrup (see page 11), guava, pineapple and mango juices, a pinch of cinnamon, and a pinch of freshly grated nutmeg. Experiment with the proportions until you find a flavor that you like.

Rickey

The classic version of this cocktail is based on gin, but other spirits are also used, mixed with lime or lemon juice and club soda with no sweetening.

serves 1

4–6 cracked ice cubes
2 measures gin
1 measure lime juice
club soda, to top off
slice of lemon, to decorate

❶ Put the cracked ice cubes into a chilled highball glass or goblet. Pour the gin and lime juice over the ice. Top off with club soda.

❷ Stir gently to mix and decorate with the lemon slice.

Variations

Whiskey Rickey: substitute American blended whiskey for the gin and decorate with a slice of lime.

Sloe Gin Rickey: substitute sloe gin for the dry gin. Decorate with a slice of lime.

Apple Rum Rickey: put 4–6 cracked ice cubes into a cocktail shaker. Pour 1 measure apple brandy, ½ measure white rum, and ½ measure lime juice over the ice and shake vigorously until a frost forms. Half fill a chilled glass with cracked ice cubes and strain the cocktail over them. Top off with sparkling mineral water and decorate with a lime twist.

Kirsch Rickey: half fill a chilled glass with cracked ice cubes. Pour 2 measures kirsch and 1 tablespoon lime juice over the ice. Top off with sparkling mineral water and stir gently. Decorate with pitted fresh cherries.

Singapore Sling

In the days of the British Empire, the privileged would gather in the relative cool of the evening to refresh parched throats and gossip about the day's events at exclusive clubs. Those days are long gone, but a Singapore Sling is still the ideal thirst-quencher on hot evenings.

serves 1

10–12 cracked ice cubes
2 measures gin
1 measure cherry brandy
1 measure lemon juice
1 tsp grenadine
club soda, to top off

To decorate

lime peel
cocktail cherries

❶ Put 4–6 cracked ice cubes into a cocktail shaker. Pour the gin, cherry brandy, lemon juice, and grenadine over the ice. Shake vigorously until a frost forms.

❷ Half fill a chilled highball glass with cracked ice cubes and strain the cocktail over them. Top off with club soda and then decorate with a twist of lime peel and cocktail cherries.

Variations

Sweet Singapore Sling: put 4–6 cracked ice cubes into a cocktail shaker. Dash lemon juice over the ice and pour in 1 measure gin and 2 measures cherry brandy. Shake vigorously until a frost forms. Half fill a chilled glass with cracked ice cubes and strain the cocktail over them. Top off with club soda and decorate with cocktail cherries.

Gin Sling: put 1 teaspoon sugar in a mixing glass. Add 1 measure lemon juice and 1 teaspoon water and stir until the sugar has dissolved. Pour in 2 measures gin and stir to mix. Half fill a small, chilled glass with ice and strain the cocktail over it. Decorate with an orange peel twist.

Whiskey Sling: put 1 teaspoon sugar in a mixing glass. Add 1 measure lemon juice and 1 teaspoon water and stir until the sugar has dissolved. Pour in 2 measures American blended whiskey and stir to mix. Half fill a small, chilled glass with ice and strain the cocktail over it. Decorate with an orange peel twist.

Long Island Iced Tea

Like many other classics, this cocktail dates from the days of Prohibition, when it was drunk from tea cups in an unconvincing attempt to fool the FBI that it was a harmless beverage. It started out life as a simple combination of vodka colored with a dash of cola, but has evolved into a more elaborate, but no less potent, concoction.

serves 1

10–12 cracked ice cubes

2 measures vodka

1 measure gin

1 measure white tequila

1 measure white rum

½ measure white crème de menthe

2 measures lemon juice

1 tsp sugar syrup (see page 11)

cola, to top off

wedge of lime or lemon, to decorate

❶ Put 4–6 cracked ice cubes into a cocktail shaker. Pour the vodka, gin, tequila, rum, crème de menthe, lemon juice, and sugar syrup over the ice. Shake vigorously until a frost forms.

❷ Half fill a tall, chilled Collins glass with cracked ice cubes and strain the cocktail over them. Top off with cola and decorate with the lime or lemon wedge.

Brewing up

Artillery Punch (serves 30): pour 4 cups bourbon, 4 cups red wine, 4 cups strong, black tea, scant 2 cups dark rum, 1 cup gin, 4 cups apricot brandy, 4 measures lemon juice, 4 measures lime juice, and 4 tablespoons sugar syrup (see page 11) in a large bowl. Refrigerate for at least 2 hours. To serve, place a large block of ice in a punch bowl or large serving bowl. Pour the punch over the ice and decorate with thinly sliced lemon and lime.

Did you know?

In 1920, there were about 15,000 bars in New York. Following the introduction of Prohibition in 1920, the number of illegal speakeasies rocketed to about 32,000.

Dubarry

The Comtesse du Barry, the mistress of King Louis XV of France, was renowned for her extraordinary beauty. The guillotine brought an abrupt ending to her life—be careful not to lose your head over this delicious concoction.

serves 1

4-6 cracked ice cubes
dash of Pernod
dash of Angostura bitters
2 measures gin
1 measure dry vermouth
lemon peel twist, to decorate

❶ Put the ice cubes into a mixing glass and dash the Pernod and Angostura bitters over them. Pour in the gin and vermouth and stir well to mix.

❷ Strain into a chilled cocktail or wine glass and decorate with a twist of lemon.

Royal connections

Nell Gwynn: put 4-6 cracked ice cubes into a mixing glass. Pour 1 measure triple sec, 1 measure peach schnapps, and 1 measure white crème de menthe over the ice, and stir well to mix. Strain into a chilled cocktail glass and decorate with an orange peel twist.

Wallis Simpson: pour 1 measure Southern Comfort into a chilled champagne flute, add 1 teaspoon superfine sugar, and stir well until dissolved. Add a dash of Angostura bitters and top off with chilled champagne. Decorate with an orange slice.

Not Tonight Joséphine: put 4-6 cracked ice cubes into a mixing glass. Pour 1 measure Mandarine Napoléon, 1 measure Campari, and 1 measure brandy over the ice, and stir well. Strain into a chilled champagne flute and top off with chilled champagne.

Mrs. Fitzherbert: put 4-6 cracked ice cubes into a mixing glass. Pour 1 measure white port and 1 measure cherry brandy over the ice and then stir until mixed well. Strain the mixture into a chilled cocktail glass.

Maiden's Blush

The name of this cocktail aptly describes its pretty color. Too many, however, and maidenly modesty may be abandoned and blushing could become compulsory.

serves 1

4–6 cracked ice cubes

2 measures gin

½ tsp triple sec

½ tsp grenadine

½ tsp lemon juice

❶ Put the cracked ice cubes into a cocktail shaker. Pour the gin, triple sec, grenadine, and lemon juice over the ice. Shake vigorously until a frost forms.
❷ Strain into a chilled cocktail glass or small highball glass.

Marital status

Maidenly Blush: put 4–6 cracked ice cubes into a mixing glass. Pour 2 measures gin and 1 measure Pernod over the ice. Stir well to mix, then strain into a chilled cocktail glass.

Maiden's Prayer: put 4–6 cracked ice cubes into a cocktail shaker. Pour 1 measure gin, 1 measure triple sec, 1 teaspoon orange juice, and 1 teaspoon lemon juice over the ice. Shake vigorously until a frost forms, then strain into a chilled cocktail glass.

Virgin's Prayer: put 4–6 cracked ice cubes into a cocktail shaker. Pour 1 measure white rum, 1 measure dark rum, 1 measure Kahlúa, 1 teaspoon lemon juice, and 2 teaspoons orange juice over the ice. Shake vigorously until a frost forms, then strain into a small, chilled glass. Decorate with slices of lime.

Wedding Belle: put 4–6 cracked ice cubes into a cocktail shaker. Pour 2 measures gin, 2 measures Dubonnet, 1 measure cherry brandy, and 1 measure orange juice over the ice. Shake until a frost forms, then strain into a cocktail glass.

Widow's Wish: put 4–6 cracked ice cubes into a mixing glass. Pour 2 measures Bénédictine over the ice and add 1 egg. Shake vigorously until a frost forms, then strain into a chilled glass. Top off with light cream.

Bartender's Tip
For a Bride's Mother, see page 94.

Piña Colada

One of the younger generation of classics, this became popular during the cocktail revival of the 1980s and has remained so ever since.

serves 1

4–6 crushed ice cubes

2 measures white rum

1 measure dark rum

3 measures pineapple juice

2 measures coconut cream

pineapple wedges, to decorate

❶ Put the crushed ice into a blender and add the white rum, dark rum, pineapple juice, and coconut cream. Blend until smooth.

❷ Pour, without straining, into a tall, chilled glass and decorate with pineapple wedges speared on a cocktail stick.

Variations

Lighten Up Piña Colada: put 4–6 cracked ice cubes into a cocktail shaker. Pour 2 measures white rum, 2 measures Malibu, and 3 measures pineapple juice over the ice. Shake vigorously until a frost forms. Half fill a small, chilled glass with cracked ice cubes. Strain the cocktail over them. Decorate with a pineapple slice.

Amigos Piña Colada (to serve 4): put 10–12 crushed ice cubes into a blender and add 1 cup white rum, 1¼ cups pineapple juice, 5 measures coconut cream, 2 measures dark rum, and 2 measures light cream. Blend until smooth. Pour, without straining, into long, chilled glasses and decorate with pineapple wedges speared on cocktail sticks.

Strawberry Colada: put 4–6 crushed ice cubes into a blender and add 3 measures golden rum, 4 measures pineapple juice, 1 measure coconut cream, and 6 hulled strawberries. Blend until smooth, then pour, without straining, into a tall, chilled glass. Decorate with pineapple wedges and strawberries speared on a cocktail stick.

Banana Colada: put 4–6 crushed ice cubes into a blender and add 2 measures white rum, 4 measures pineapple juice, 1 measure Malibu, and 1 peeled and sliced banana. Blend until smooth, then pour, without straining, into a tall, chilled glass and serve with a straw.

Acapulco

This is one of many cocktails that has changed from its original recipe over the years. To begin with, it was always rum-based and did not include any fruit juice. Nowadays, it is increasingly made with tequila, because this has become better known outside its native Mexico.

serves 1

10–12 cracked ice cubes

2 measures white rum

½ measure triple sec

½ measure lime juice

1 tsp sugar syrup (see page 11)

1 egg white

sprig of fresh mint, to decorate

❶ Put 4–6 cracked ice cubes into a cocktail shaker. Pour the rum, triple sec, lime juice, and sugar syrup over the ice, and add the egg white. Shake vigorously until a frost forms.

❷ Half fill a chilled highball glass with cracked ice cubes and strain the cocktail over them. Decorate with the mint sprig.

Variations

Tequila Acapulco: put 4–6 cracked ice cubes into a cocktail shaker. Pour 1 measure white tequila, 1 measure white rum, 4 measures pineapple juice, and 1 measure lime juice over the ice. Shake vigorously until a frost forms. Hall fill a small, chilled glass with cracked ice cubes and strain the cocktail over them.

Acapulco Gold: put 4–6 cracked ice cubes into a cocktail shaker and add 1 measure golden tequila, 1 measure golden rum, 2 measures pineapple juice, 1 measure coconut cream, and 1 measure grapefruit juice. Shake until a frost forms. Half fill a chilled glass with cracked ice cubes and strain the cocktail over them.

Did you know?

Rum owes its origin to Christopher Columbus, who is said to have planted the first sugar cane in the islands of the Caribbean.

Daiquiri

Daiquiri is a town in Cuba, where this drink was said to have been invented in the early part of the twentieth century. A businessman had run out of imported gin, so he had to make do with the local drink—rum—which, at that time, was of unreliable quality. To ensure that his guests would find it palatable, he decided to mix it with other ingredients. This classic has since given rise to almost innumerable variations.

serves 1

4–6 cracked ice cubes
2 measures white rum
¾ measure lime juice
½ tsp sugar syrup (see page 11)

❶ Put the cracked ice cubes into a cocktail shaker. Pour the rum, lime juice, and sugar syrup over the ice. Shake vigorously until a frost forms.
❷ Strain into a chilled cocktail glass.

Variations

Derby Daiquiri: put 4–6 crushed ice cubes into a blender and add 2 measures white rum, 1 measure orange juice, ½ measure triple sec, and ½ measure lime juice. Blend until smooth, then pour, without straining, into a chilled cocktail glass.

Banana Daiquiri: put 4–6 crushed ice cubes into a blender and then add 2 measures white rum, ½ measure triple sec, ½ measure lime juice, ½ measure light cream, 1 teaspoon sugar syrup (see page 11), and ¼ peeled and sliced banana. Blend until smooth, then pour the mixture, without straining, into a chilled goblet and decorate it with a slice of lime.

Peach Daiquiri: put 4–6 crushed ice cubes into a blender and add 2 measures white rum, 1 measure lime juice, ½ teaspoon sugar syrup (see page 11) and ½ peeled, pitted, and chopped peach. Blend until smooth, then pour, without straining, into a chilled goblet.

Passionate Daiquiri: put 4–6 cracked ice cubes into a cocktail shaker. Pour 2 measures white rum, 1 measure lime juice, and ½ measure passion fruit syrup over the ice. Shake vigorously until a frost forms. Strain into a chilled cocktail glass and decorate with a cocktail cherry.

Bartender's Tip
For other Daiquiri variations, see page 150.

Planter's Punch

Derived from a Hindi word meaning five, punch is so called because, traditionally, it contained five ingredients. These should also include four basic flavors—strong, weak, sour, and sweet.

serves 1

10–12 cracked ice cubes

dash of grenadine

2 measures white rum

2 measures dark rum

1 measure lemon juice

1 measure lime juice

1 tsp sugar syrup (see page 11)

¼ tsp triple sec

sparkling mineral water, to top off

To decorate

slice of lemon

slice of lime

slice of pineapple

cocktail cherry

❶ Put 4–6 cracked ice cubes into a cocktail shaker. Dash the grenadine over the ice and pour in the white rum, dark rum, lemon juice, lime juice, sugar syrup, and triple sec. Shake vigorously until a frost forms.

❷ Half fill a tall, chilled Collins glass with cracked ice cubes and strain the cocktail over them. Top off with sparkling mineral water and stir gently. Decorate with the lemon, lime, and pineapple slices, and a cherry.

Variations

Plantation Punch: put 4–6 cracked ice cubes into a cocktail shaker. Pour 2 measures dark rum, 1 measure Southern Comfort, and 1 measure lemon juice over the ice, and add 1 teaspoon brown sugar. Shake vigorously until a frost forms. Strain into a tall, chilled glass and top off, almost to the rim, with sparkling mineral water. Float 1 teaspoon of ruby port on top by pouring it gently over the back of a teaspoon and garnish with a lemon slice and an orange slice.

Planter's Cocktail: put 4–6 cracked ice cubes into a cocktail shaker. Dash lemon juice over the ice and pour in 1 measure rum and 1 measure orange juice. Shake vigorously until a frost forms, then strain into a chilled cocktail glass.

Cuba Libre

The 1960s and 1970s saw the meteoric rise in popularity of this simple, long drink, perhaps because of highly successful marketing by Bacardi brand rum, the original white Cuban rum (now produced in the Bahamas) and Coca-Cola, but more likely because rum and cola seem to be natural companions.

serves 1

4-6 cracked ice cubes
2 measures white rum
cola, to top off
wedge of lime, to decorate

❶ Half fill a highball glass with cracked ice cubes. Pour the rum over the ice and top off with cola.

❷ Stir gently to mix and decorate with a lime wedge.

Other Cuban classics

Cuban Special: put 4-6 cracked ice cubes into a cocktail shaker. Pour 2 measures rum, 1 measure lime juice, 1 tablespoon pineapple juice, and 1 teaspoon triple sec over the ice. Shake vigorously until a frost forms. Strain into a chilled cocktail glass and decorate with a pineapple wedge.

Bacardi Cocktail: put 4-6 cracked ice cubes into a cocktail shaker. Pour 2 measures Bacardi rum, 1 measure grenadine, and 1 measure fresh lime juice over the ice. Shake vigorously until a frost forms. Strain into a chilled cocktail glass.

Cuban: put 4-6 cracked ice cubes into a cocktail shaker. Pour 2 measures brandy, 1 measure apricot brandy, 1 measure lime juice, and 1 teaspoon white rum over the ice. Shake vigorously until a frost forms. Strain into a chilled cocktail glass.

Brandy Cuban: half fill a chilled glass with cracked ice cubes. Pour 1½ measures brandy, and ½ measure lime juice over the ice. Top off with cola and stir gently. Decorate with a slice of lime.

Did you know?

Britain's Royal Navy continued to provide sailors with a daily rum ration until 1969 although, by then, the quantity had been reduced from the original 1¼ cups.

Zombie

The individual ingredients of this cocktail, including liqueurs and fruit juices, vary considerably from one recipe to another, but all zombies contain a mixture of white, golden, and dark rum in a range of proportions.

serves 1

4–6 crushed ice cubes
2 measures dark rum
2 measures white rum
1 measure golden rum
1 measure triple sec
1 measure lime juice
1 measure orange juice
1 measure pineapple juice
1 measure guava juice
1 tbsp grenadine
1 tbsp orgeat
1 tsp Pernod

To decorate

sprig of fresh mint
pineapple wedges

❶ Put the crushed ice cubes into a blender and add the three rums, triple sec, lime juice, orange juice, pineapple juice, guava juice, grenadine, orgeat, and Pernod. Blend until smooth.

❷ Pour, without straining, into a chilled Collins glass and decorate with the mint sprig and pineapple wedges.

Variations

Walking Zombie: put 4–6 cracked ice cubes into a cocktail shaker. Pour 1 measure white rum, 1 measure golden rum, 1 measure dark rum, 1 measure apricot brandy, 1 measure lime juice, 1 measure pineapple juice, and 1 teaspoon sugar syrup (see page 11) over the ice. Shake vigorously until a frost forms. Half fill a chilled glass with cracked ice cubes and strain the cocktail over them. Decorate with orange and lemon slices.

Bartender's Tip
Orgeat is an almond-flavored syrup. If you can't find it, you could substitute the same amount of amaretto, which is more widely available.

Mai Tai

For some reason, this cocktail always inspires elaborate decoration with paper parasols, a selection of fruit, and spirals of citrus rind—sometimes so much so that you can be in danger of stabbing your nose on a cocktail stick when you try to drink it. If you want to go wild with decorations—and why not—serving the drink with one or two long, colorful straws might be a good idea.

serves 1

4–6 cracked ice cubes

2 measures white rum

2 measures dark rum

1 measure clear Curaçao

1 measure lime juice

1 tbsp orgeat

1 tbsp grenadine

To decorate

paper parasol

slices of pineapple

cocktail cherries

orchid, optional

❶ Put the cracked ice cubes into a cocktail shaker. Pour the white and dark rums, Curaçao, lime juice, orgeat, and grenadine over the ice. Shake vigorously until a frost forms.

❷ Strain into a chilled Collins glass and decorate with the paper parasol, pineapple, and cherries, adding an orchid, if desired.

Other decorated cocktails

Generally speaking, you can decorate cocktails in any way you like—or not at all, if you prefer. There are some, however, that are traditionally served in a particular way. The Martini and the Gibson (see page 40), for example, are differentiated only because the former is decorated with a cocktail olive, while the latter is always served with a cocktail onion.

Horse's Neck: hang a long spiral of lemon rind over the rim of a tall, chilled glass. Fill the glass with cracked ice and pour 2 measures American blended whiskey over the ice. Top off with ginger ale and stir.

Ultimate Beefeater Martini: put 4–6 cracked ice cubes into a mixing glass. Dash dry vermouth over the ice and pour in 1 measure Beefeater gin. Stir well to mix and strain the mixture into a chilled cocktail glass. Decorate with a sliver of fillet steak.

Margarita

The traditional way to drink tequila is to shake a little salt on the back of your hand between the thumb and forefinger and, holding a wedge of lime or lemon, lick the salt, suck the fruit, and then down a shot of tequila in one. This cocktail, attributed to Francisco Morales and invented in 1942 in Mexico, is a more civilized version.

serves 1

lime wedge

coarse salt

4–6 cracked ice cubes

3 measures white tequila

1 measure triple sec

2 measures lime juice

slice of lime, to decorate

❶ Rub the rim of a chilled cocktail glass with the lime wedge and then dip in a saucer of coarse salt to frost.

❷ Put the cracked ice cubes into a cocktail shaker. Pour the tequila, triple sec, and lime juice over the ice. Shake vigorously until a frost forms.

❸ Strain into the prepared glass and decorate with the lime slice.

Variations

Frozen Margarita: put 6–8 cracked ice cubes into a blender and add 2 measures white tequila, 1 measure lime juice, and ½ measure triple sec. Blend at low speed until slushy. Pour, without straining, into a chilled cocktail glass and decorate with a slice of lime.

Blue Margarita: frost the rim of a chilled cocktail glass using a lime wedge and coarse salt (as above). Put 4–6 cracked ice cubes into a cocktail shaker. Pour 2 measures white tequila, 1 measure blue Curaçao, 1½ measures lime juice, and 1 tablespoon triple sec over the ice. Shake until a frost forms. Strain into the prepared glass. Decorate with a slice of lime.

5757 Gin Margarita (from the bar of the same name in the Four Seasons Hotel, New York City): put 4–6 cracked ice cubes into a cocktail shaker. Pour 1½ measures gin, ½ measure triple sec, and 1 measure lemon juice over the ice, and add sugar syrup (see page 11) to taste. Shake vigorously until a frost forms, then strain into a chilled cocktail glass.

Margarita Impériale: put 4–6 cracked ice cubes into a cocktail shaker. Dash clear Curaçao over the ice and pour in 1 measure white tequila, 1 measure Mandarine Napoléon, and 1 measure lemon juice. Shake vigorously until a frost forms. Strain into a chilled cocktail glass.

Tequila Sunrise

This is one cocktail you shouldn't rush when making, otherwise you will spoil the attractive sunrise effect as the grenadine slowly spreads through the orange juice.

serves 1

4–6 cracked ice cubes
2 parts white tequila
orange juice, to top off
1 measure grenadine

❶ Put the cracked ice cubes into a chilled highball glass. Pour the tequila over the ice and top off with the orange juice. Stir well to mix.
❷ Slowly pour in the grenadine and serve with a straw.

Variations

Blinding Sunrise: put 4–6 cracked ice cubes into a cocktail shaker. Pour 1 measure white tequila, 1 measure vodka, 3 measures orange juice, and 1 teaspoon triple sec over the ice. Shake until a frost forms. Half fill a glass with cracked ice cubes and strain the cocktail over them. Slowly pour in 1 measure grenadine.

Pacific Sunrise: put 4–6 cracked ice cubes into a cocktail shaker. Dash Angostura bitters over the ice and pour in 1 measure white tequila, 1 measure blue Curaçao, and 1 measure lime juice. Shake vigorously until a frost forms, then strain into a chilled cocktail glass.

Mint Sunrise: put 4–6 cracked ice cubes into a chilled glass. Pour 1½ measures Scotch whisky, ½ measure brandy, and ½ measure clear Curaçao over the ice and stir gently. Decorate with a fresh mint sprig and a slice of lemon.

Bartender's Tip

For a nonalcoholic Sunrise, see page 230.

Did you know?

The popularity of tequila took producers by surprise. The agave plant from which it is made takes 8–10 years to mature: slow maturation and cultivation problems created a severe shortage by the year 2000, which resulted in rocketing prices and a lucrative trade in "cactus rustling".

Brave Bull

Spain's historical associations with Mexico have left many legacies—not least a taste for bullfighting—although whether this cocktail is named in tribute to the animal or because it makes the drinker proverbially brave is anyone's guess.

serves 1

4-6 cracked ice cubes
2 measures white tequila
1 measure Tia Maria
spiral of lemon peel, to decorate

❶ Put the cracked ice into a mixing glass. Pour the tequila and Tia Maria over the ice and stir well to mix.
❷ Strain into a chilled goblet and decorate with the lemon peel spiral.

Olé!

Matador: put 4-6 cracked ice cubes into a cocktail shaker. Pour 1 measure white tequila, 2 measures pineapple juice, and 1 measure lime juice over the ice. Shake until a frost forms. Fill a chilled glass with cracked ice and strain the cocktail over it.

Frozen Matador: put 4-6 crushed ice cubes into a blender and add 2 measures golden tequila, 2 measures pineapple juice, and ½ measure lime juice. Blend until smooth and pour into a chilled goblet. Decorate with a slice of lime.

Toreador: put 4-6 cracked ice cubes into a cocktail shaker. Pour 2 measures white tequila, ½ measure white crème de cacao, and ½ measure light cream over the ice. Shake vigorously until a frost forms. Strain into a chilled cocktail glass.

Bull's Milk: put 4-6 cracked ice cubes into a mixing glass. Pour 2 measures brandy, 1 measure dark rum, ⅔ cup milk, and ½ teaspoon sugar syrup (see page 11) over the ice, and stir well to mix. Pour, without straining, into a chilled glass and sprinkle the cocktail with freshly grated nutmeg.

Blood and Sand: put 4-6 cracked ice cubes into a cocktail shaker. Pour 1 measure Scotch whisky, ½ measure cherry brandy, ½ measure sweet vermouth, and ½ measure orange juice over the ice. Shake vigorously until a frost forms. Strain into a chilled cocktail glass.

Bartender's Tip
For a Royal Matador, see page 154.

Bloody Mary

This classic cocktail was invented in 1921 at the legendary Harry's Bar in Paris. There are numerous versions—some much hotter and spicier than others. Ingredients may include horseradish sauce in addition to or instead of Tabasco sauce, more or less tomato juice, and lime juice instead of lemon. Sometimes the glass is decorated with a sprig of mint. Whatever the version, all experts agree that it is essential to use the highest-quality ingredients.

serves 1

4–6 cracked ice cubes
dash of Worcestershire sauce
dash of Tabasco sauce
2 measures vodka
6 measures tomato juice
juice of ½ lemon
pinch of celery salt
pinch of cayenne pepper

To decorate
celery stalk with leaves
slice of lemon

❶ Put the cracked ice into a cocktail shaker. Dash the Worcestershire sauce and Tabasco sauce over the ice and pour in the vodka, tomato juice, and lemon juice. Shake vigorously until a frost forms.
❷ Strain into a chilled glass, add a pinch of celery salt and a pinch of cayenne, and decorate with a celery stalk and a slice of lemon.

Variations

Bloody Maria: substitute 2 measures white tequila for the vodka and add 1 teaspoon horseradish sauce, and a pinch of ground coriander. Decorate with a lime wedge.

Cold and Clammy Bloody Mary: substitute 3 measures clam juice for 3 of the measures of tomato juice and decorate with a scallion curl.

Bullshot: substitute 4 measures chilled beef bouillon for the tomato juice. Season with salt and freshly ground black pepper.

Ginza Mary: put 4–6 cracked ice cubes into a mixing glass. Dash Tabasco sauce and soy sauce over the ice and pour in 2 measures vodka, 1½ measures sake, 2 measures tomato juice, and ½ measure lemon juice. Season to taste with freshly ground black pepper. Stir well. Pour, without straining, into a chilled glass.

Bartender's Tip

For a Bloody January and other non-alcoholic variations, see page 220.

Mojito cocktail
                    3 cups
Rum — 750 mel.
evapor. milk — 3 o oz.
cream of coco (coco lopez) 1 can
Condense milk 1 can
put in blender
refrig for 2 days
c̄ two cinnamon
sticks · ·
Serve on crushed
ice —
good sutestitute
for eggnog

Black Russian

History records only White and Red Russians. The omission of the Black Russian is a sad oversight. For a coffee liqueur, you can use either Tia Maria or Kahlúa, depending on your personal taste—the latter is sweeter.

serves 1

4-6 cracked ice cubes
2 measures vodka
1 measure coffee liqueur

❶ Put the cracked ice cubes into a small, chilled highball glass. Pour the vodka and liqueur over the ice. Stir to mix.

The Russian Empire

Tall Black Russian: make a black Russian in a glass and top off with cola.

Cream Russian: put 4-6 cracked ice cubes into a cocktail shaker. Pour 2 measures vodka, 1 measure coffee liqueur, and 1 measure light cream over the ice. Shake vigorously until a frost forms. Pour, without straining, into a small, chilled glass.

White Russian: put 4-6 cracked ice cubes into a mixing glass. Pour 2 measures vodka and 1 measure white crème de menthe over the ice. Stir well and strain into a chilled cocktail glass.

Russian: put 4-6 cracked ice cubes into a mixing glass. Pour 1 measure vodka, 1 measure gin, and 1 measure white crème de cacao over the ice. Stir to mix thoroughly and strain into a chilled cocktail glass.

Russian Bear: put 4-6 cracked ice cubes into a cocktail shaker. Pour 2 measures vodka, 1 measure dark crème de cacao, and ½ measure light cream over the ice. Shake vigorously until a frost forms. Strain into a chilled cocktail glass.

Yeltsin: put 4-6 cracked ice cubes into a mixing glass. Pour 2 measures vodka, 1 measure dry vermouth, and 1 measure medium sherry over the ice. Stir well and strain into a chilled cocktail glass. Squeeze lemon peel over.

Moscow Mule

This cocktail came into existence through a happy coincidence during the 1930s. An American bar owner had overstocked ginger beer, and a representative of a soda company invented the Moscow Mule to help him out.

serves 1

10–12 cracked ice cubes
2 measures vodka
1 measure lime juice
ginger beer, to top off
slice of lime, to decorate

❶ Put 4–6 cracked ice cubes into a cocktail shaker. Pour the vodka and lime juice over the ice. Shake vigorously until a frost forms.

❷ Half fill a chilled highball glass with cracked ice cubes and strain the cocktail over them. Top off with ginger beer. Decorate with a slice of lime.

Other Stubborn Drinks

Delft Donkey: make a Moscow Mule but substitute gin for the vodka.

Mississippi Mule: put 4–6 cracked ice cubes into a cocktail shaker. Pour 2 measures gin, ½ measure crème de cassis, and ½ measure lemon juice over the ice. Shake vigorously until a frost forms, then strain into a small, chilled glass.

Mule's Hind Leg: put 4–6 cracked ice cubes into a cocktail shaker. Pour in ½ measure apricot brandy, ½ measure apple brandy, ½ measure Bénédictine, ½ measure gin, and ½ measure maple syrup. Shake vigorously until a frost forms, then strain into a chilled cocktail glass.

Jamaica Mule: put 4–6 cracked ice cubes into a cocktail shaker. Pour 2 measures white rum, 1 measure dark rum, 1 measure golden rum, 1 measure Falernum, and 1 measure lime juice over the ice. Shake vigorously until a frost forms, then strain the mixture into a tall, chilled glass. Top off with ginger beer and then decorate with some pineapple wedges and pieces of candied ginger.

Bartender's Tip

For a nonalcoholic Delirious Donkey, see page 222.

Screwdriver

Always use freshly squeezed orange juice to make this refreshing cocktail—it is just not the same with bottled juice. This simple, classic cocktail has given rise to numerous and increasingly elaborate variations.

serves 1

6–8 cracked ice cubes
2 measures vodka
orange juice, to top off
slice of orange, to decorate

❶ Fill a chilled highball glass with cracked ice cubes. Pour the vodka over the ice and top off with orange juice.
❷ Stir well to mix and decorate with a slice of orange.

Variations

Cordless Screwdriver: pour 2 measures chilled vodka into a shot glass. Dip a wedge of orange into superfine sugar. Down the vodka in one go and suck the orange.

Creamy Screwdriver: put 4–6 crushed ice cubes into a blender. Add 2 measures vodka, 6 measures orange juice, 1 egg yolk, and ½ teaspoon sugar syrup (see page 11). Blend until smooth. Half fill a chilled glass with cracked ice cubes and pour the cocktail over them without straining.

Harvey Wallbanger: make a Screwdriver and then float 1 measure Galliano on top by pouring it gently over the back of a teaspoon.

Slow Screw: substitute sloe gin for the vodka.

Bartender's Tip

Galliano is a honey- and vanilla-flavored liqueur from Italy. It is sold in tall, thin bottles, so bars store it on a top shelf up against the wall to avoid knocking it over.

Did you know?

The Harvey Wallbanger is named after a California surfer who took such prodigious delight in drinking Screwdrivers topped with a Galliano float that he ricocheted from wall to wall on leaving the bar.

Salty Dog

This is another cocktail that has changed since its invention. When it first appeared, gin-based cocktails were by far the most popular, but nowadays, a Salty Dog is more frequently made with vodka. You can use either spirit, but the cocktails will have different flavors.

serves 1

1 tbsp granulated sugar
1 tbsp coarse salt
lime wedge
6–8 cracked ice cubes
2 measures vodka
grapefruit juice, to top off

❶ Mix the sugar and salt in a saucer. Rub the rim of a chilled Collins glass with the lime wedge, then dip it in the sugar and salt mixture to frost.

❷ Fill the glass with cracked ice cubes and pour the vodka over them. Top off with grapefruit juice and stir to mix. Serve with a straw.

Variations

Bride's Mother: put 4–6 cracked ice cubes into a cocktail shaker. Pour 1½ measures sloe gin, 1 measure gin, 2½ measures grapefruit juice, and ½ measure sugar syrup (see page 11) over the ice. Shake vigorously until a frost forms, then strain into a chilled cocktail glass.

A. J: put 4–6 cracked ice cubes into a cocktail shaker. Pour 1½ measures applejack or apple brandy, and 1 measure grapefruit juice over the ice. Shake vigorously until a frost forms, then strain into a chilled cocktail glass.

Midnight Sun: put 4–6 cracked ice cubes into a cocktail shaker. Pour 2 measures aquavit, 1 measure grapefruit juice, and ¼ teaspoon grenadine over the ice. Shake vigorously until a frost forms, then strain

into a chilled cocktail glass. Decorate with a slice of orange.

Blinker: put 4–6 cracked ice cubes into a cocktail shaker. Pour 2 measures rye whiskey, 2½ measures grapefruit juice, and 1 teaspoon grenadine over the ice. Shake vigorously until a frost forms, then strain into a chilled cocktail glass.

Woodward: put 4–6 cracked ice cubes into a cocktail shaker. Pour 2 measures Scotch whisky, ½ measure dry vermouth, and ½ measure grapefruit juice over the ice. Shake vigorously until a frost forms, then strain the mixture into a chilled cocktail glass.

Bartender's Tip
For a non-alcoholic Salty Puppy, see page 230.

Grasshopper

This silky smooth, pale-green cocktail is enough to make anyone jump with delight. However, experts disagree on the original recipe and there seem to be at least three versions with the same name—as well as numerous variations. The recipe given here is also known as a Grasshopper Surprise.

serves 1

4–6 cracked ice cubes
2 measures green crème de menthe
2 measures white crème de cacao
2 measures light cream

❶ Put the cracked ice cubes into a cocktail shaker. Pour the crème de menthe, crème de cacao, and light cream over the ice. Shake vigorously until a frost forms.
❷ Strain into a chilled goblet.

Variations

Grasshopper (second version): substitute white crème de menthe for the crème de cacao.

Grasshopper (third version, also known as a Flying Grasshopper): put 4–6 cracked ice cubes into a cocktail shaker. Pour 2 measures vodka, 1 measure green crème de menthe, and 1 measure white crème de menthe over the ice. Shake vigorously until a frost forms. Strain into a chilled cocktail glass.

Coffee Grasshopper: put 4–6 cracked ice cubes into a cocktail shaker. Pour 1 measure white crème de menthe, 1½ measures coffee liqueur, and 1 measure light cream over the ice. Shake vigorously until a frost forms. Half fill a small, chilled glass with ice and strain the cocktail over it.

Vodka Grasshopper: put 4–6 cracked ice cubes into a cocktail shaker. Pour 2 measures vodka, 2 measures green crème de menthe, and 2 measures white crème de cacao over the ice. Shake vigorously until a frost forms, then strain into a chilled cocktail glass.

Rhett Butler

When Margaret Mitchell wrote her long civil war story, *Gone With the Wind*, she created an enduring romantic hero in Rhett Butler. His debonair charm and devil-may-care lifestyle were brought alive by the heart-throb movie star Clark Gable.

serves 1

4-6 cracked ice cubes
2 measures Southern Comfort
½ measure clear Curaçao
½ measure lime juice
1 tsp lemon juice
twist of lemon peel, to decorate

❶ Put the cracked ice cubes into a cocktail shaker. Pour the Southern Comfort, Curaçao, lime juice, and lemon juice over the ice. Shake vigorously until a frost forms.

❷ Strain into a chilled cocktail glass and decorate with the lemon twist.

"Tomorrow is another day"

Scarlett O'Hara: put 4-6 cracked ice cubes into a cocktail shaker. Pour 2 measures Southern Comfort, 2 measures cranberry juice, and 1 measure lime juice over the ice. Shake vigorously until a frost forms, then strain into a chilled cocktail glass.

Ashley Wilkes: crush 3 fresh mint sprigs and place in a chilled glass. Add 1 teaspoon sugar, a dash of lime juice, and 6 cracked ice cubes. Pour in 2 measures bourbon and 1 measure peach brandy and stir to mix. Decorate with a fresh sprig of mint.

Melanie Hamilton: put 4-6 cracked ice cubes into a cocktail shaker. Pour 2 measures triple sec, 1 measure Midori, and 2 measures orange juice over the ice. Shake vigorously until a frost forms, then strain into a chilled cocktail glass. Decorate with a wedge of cantaloupe melon.

Absinthe Friend

A popular cocktail ingredient, the *digestif* absinthe is no longer available. Flavored with wormwood, which it is said reacts with alcohol to cause brain damage, absinthe was banned by law in 1915. However, various pastis, including Pernod and Ricard, are still available and make good substitutes.

serves 1

4–6 cracked ice cubes
dash of Angostura bitters
dash of sugar syrup (see page 11)
1 measure Pernod
1 measure gin

❶ Put the cracked ice cubes into a cocktail shaker. Dash the bitters and sugar syrup over the ice and pour in the Pernod and gin. Shake vigorously until a frost forms.
❷ Strain into a chilled glass.

Absinthe makes the heart grow fonder

Suisse: put 4–6 ice cubes into a cocktail shaker. Dash Anisette over the ice, pour in 1 measure Pernod, and add 1 egg white. Shake vigorously until a frost forms, then strain into a chilled cocktail glass.

Earthquake: put 4–6 ice cubes into a mixing glass. Pour 1 measure Pernod, 1 measure gin, and 1 measure bourbon over the ice. Stir well to mix and strain into a chilled cocktail glass.

Waldorf: put 4–6 ice cubes into a cocktail shaker. Dash Angostura bitters over the ice and pour in 1 measure Pernod, 2 measures bourbon, and ½ measure sweet vermouth. Shake until a frost forms. Strain into a chilled cocktail glass.

Yellow Parrot: put 4–6 ice cubes into a cocktail shaker. Pour 2 measures Pernod, 2 measures brandy, and 2 measures yellow Chartreuse over the ice. Shake vigorously until a frost forms. Strain into a chilled cocktail glass.

Did you know?

When absinthe was first produced in the late eighteenth century, it was marketed as an aphrodisiac.

Negroni

This aristocratic cocktail was created by Count Negroni at the Bar Giacosa in Florence, although since then, the proportions of gin to Campari have altered.

serves 1

4–6 cracked ice cubes
1 measure Campari
1 measure gin
½ measure sweet vermouth
twist of orange peel, to decorate

❶ Put the cracked ice cubes into a mixing glass. Pour the Campari, gin, and vermouth over the ice. Stir well to mix.
❷ Strain into a chilled glass and decorate with the orange twist.

The fine Italian hand

Americano: put 4–6 ice cubes into a chilled glass. Pour 1½ measures sweet vermouth, and 1½ measures Campari over the ice. Top off with club soda and stir to mix thoroughly. Decorate with a twist of lemon peel.

Italian Stallion: put 4–6 ice cubes into a mixing glass. Dash Angostura bitters over the ice and pour in 2 measures bourbon, 1 measure Campari, and ½ measure sweet vermouth. Stir well to mix, then strain into a chilled cocktail glass and decorate with a twist of lemon peel.

Genoa Vodka: put 4–6 ice cubes into a cocktail shaker. Pour 2 measures vodka, 1 measure Campari, and 3 measures orange juice over the ice. Shake vigorously until a frost forms. Strain into a chilled glass and decorate with a slice of orange.

Rosita: put 4–6 ice cubes into a mixing glass. Pour 2 measures Campari, 2 measures white tequila, ½ measure dry vermouth, and ½ measure sweet vermouth over the ice. Stir well to mix, then strain into a small, chilled glass and decorate with a twist of lemon peel.

Rolls Royce

Hardly surprisingly, several classic cocktails have been named after this classic marque. This version was created by author H. E. Bates in his popular novel *The Darling Buds of May*.

serves 1

4–6 cracked ice cubes

dash of orange bitters

2 measures dry vermouth

1 measure dry gin

1 measure Scotch whisky

❶ Put the cracked ice cubes into a mixing glass. Dash the ice with the bitters.

❷ Pour the vermouth, gin, and whisky over the ice and stir to mix. Strain into a chilled cocktail glass.

Classic Cars

Rolls Royce (second version): put 4–6 ice cubes into a glass and add 3 measures gin, 1 measure dry vermouth, 1 measure sweet vermouth, and ¼ teaspoon Bénédictine. Stir well, then strain into a chilled cocktail glass.

American Rolls Royce: put 4–6 ice cubes into a cocktail shaker. Pour 2 measures brandy, 1 measure triple sec, and 2 measures orange juice over the ice. Shake vigorously until a frost forms, then strain into a chilled cocktail glass.

Bentley: put 4–6 ice cubes into a mixing glass. Pour 2 measures Calvados and 1 measure red Dubonnet over the ice and stir. Strain the mixture into a chilled cocktail glass and decorate with a twist of lemon peel.

Golden Cadillac: put 4–6 ice cubes into a cocktail shaker. Pour 1 measure triple sec, 1 measure Galliano, and 1 measure light cream over the ice. Shake vigorously until a frost forms, then strain into a chilled cocktail glass.

Did you know?

Writers and cocktails seem to have a special affinity. Raymond Chandler wrote affectionately of the Gimlet; Scott Fitzgerald evoked the glamor of cocktail society in The Great Gatsby; *and Ian Fleming created a variation of the Martini in* Casino Royale.

Kir

As with the best mustard, crème de cassis production is centered on the French city of Dijon. This cocktail is named in commemoration of a partisan and mayor of the city, Félix Kir.

serves 1

4–6 cracked ice cubes
2 measures crème de cassis
white wine, to top off
twist of lemon peel, to decorate

❶ Put the crushed ice cubes into a chilled wine glass. Pour the crème de cassis over the ice.

❷ Top off with chilled white wine and stir well. Decorate with the lemon twist.

Wine toppers

Kir Royale: substitute champagne for the white wine.

Osborne (named after Queen Victoria's Isle of Wight residence and apparently a favorite tipple of Her Majesty's): pour 3 measures claret and 1 measure Scotch whisky into a goblet and stir to mix.

Bellini (created at Harry's Bar, Venice, and named after the Renaissance artist): fill a goblet with crushed ice and dash over grenadine. Pour in 1 measure peach juice, then top off with chilled champagne. Decorate with a peeled, fresh peach slice.

Bellinitini: put 4–6 cracked ice cubes into a cocktail shaker. Pour in 2 measures vodka, 1 measure peach schnapps, and 1 measure peach juice. Shake until a frost forms, then strain into a chilled goblet. Top off with chilled champagne.

Rikki-Tikki-Tavi: put a sugar cube into a chilled champagne flute and dash with Angostura bitters until red but still intact. Pour in 1 teaspoon brandy and 1 teaspoon clear Curaçao and top off with chilled champagne.

Champagne Pick-me-up: put 4–6 cracked ice cubes into a cocktail shaker. Dash grenadine over the ice and pour in 2 measures brandy, 1 measure orange juice, and 1 measure lemon juice. Shake vigorously until a frost forms. Strain into a wine glass and top off with chilled champagne.

Bartender's Tip

For a nonalcoholic Faux Kir and variations, see page 226. For a nonalcoholic Baby Bellini, see page 230.

Sherry Cobbler

A long drink made with syrup and fresh fruit garnishes, Sherry Cobbler is the original, but there are now numerous and often more potent variations.

serves 1

6–8 cracked ice cubes
¼ tsp sugar syrup (see page 11)
¼ tsp clear Curaçao
4 measures Amontillado sherry

To decorate
pineapple wedges
twist of lemon peel

❶ Fill a wine glass with crushed ice. Add the sugar syrup and Curaçao and stir until a frost forms.
❷ Pour in the sherry and stir well. Decorate with pineapple wedges speared on a cocktail stick and the lemon twist.

Variations

Port Wine Cobbler: put 1 teaspoon superfine sugar into a chilled wine glass and add 2 measures sparkling mineral water. Stir until the sugar has dissolved. Fill the glass with cracked ice and pour in 3 measures ruby port. Decorate with a slice of orange and a cocktail cherry.

Champagne Cobbler: put 4–6 cracked ice cubes into a goblet. Pour 1 measure brandy and 1 measure clear Curaçao over the ice and top off with chilled champagne. Decorate with a slice of orange.

Bourbon Cobbler: put 1 teaspoon superfine sugar into a tall, chilled glass and dash lemon juice over it. Add 6 cracked ice cubes and pour in 2 measures bourbon and 2 measures Southern Comfort. Top off with club soda and stir to mix. Decorate with a peach slice.

Brandy Cobbler: put 1 teaspoon superfine sugar into a small, chilled glass and add 3 measures sparkling mineral water. Stir until the sugar has dissolved, the fill the glass with cracked ice. Pour in 2 measures brandy and stir well. Decorate with a slice of lemon and a cocktail cherry.

Rum Cobbler: put 1 teaspoon superfine sugar into a chilled goblet. Add 2 measures sparkling mineral water and stir until the sugar has dissolved. Fill the glass with cracked ice and pour in 2 measures white rum. Stir well and decorate with a lime slice and an orange slice.

French 75

Although this cocktail was described in a cocktails book written in the early twentieth century as something that "definitely hits the spot," there seems to be some confusion about the actual ingredients. All recipes include champagne, but disagree about the spirits included.

serves 1

4–6 cracked ice cubes
2 measures brandy
1 measure lemon juice
1 tbsp sugar syrup (see page 11)
chilled champagne, to top off
twist of lemon peel, to decorate

❶ Put the cracked ice cubes into a cocktail shaker. Pour the brandy, lemon juice, and sugar syrup over the ice and shake vigorously until a frost forms.

❷ Strain into a chilled highball glass and top off with champagne. Decorate with the lemon twist.

Vive la France

French 75 (second version): put 4–6 cracked ice cubes into a cocktail shaker. Pour 2 measures Plymouth gin and 1 measure lime juice over the ice and shake vigorously until a frost forms. Strain into a chilled wine glass and top off with chilled champagne. Decorate with a cocktail cherry.

French 75 (third version): put 1 teaspoon superfine sugar into a tall, chilled glass. Add 1 measure lemon juice and stir until the sugar has dissolved. Fill the glass with cracked ice cubes. Pour 2 measures gin over the ice and top off with chilled champagne. Decorate with slices of orange and cocktail cherries.

London French 75: make the second version of a French 75, but substitute London gin for the Plymouth gin and lemon juice for the lime.

French Kiss: put 4–6 ice cubes into a cocktail shaker. Pour 2 measures bourbon, 1 measure apricot liqueur, 2 teaspoons grenadine, and 1 teaspoon lemon juice over the ice. Shake vigorously until a frost forms, then strain into a chilled cocktail glass.

French Rose: put 4–6 ice cubes into a mixing glass. Pour 2 measures gin, 1 measure cherry brandy, and 1 measure dry vermouth over the ice. Stir well and strain into a chilled cocktail glass.

Buck's Fizz

Invented at Buck's Club in London, the original was invariably made with Bollinger champagne and it is true that the better the quality of the champagne, the better the flavor.

serves 1

2 measures chilled champagne
2 measures chilled orange juice

❶ Pour the champagne into a chilled champagne flute, then pour in the orange juice.

Variations

Duck's Fizz: substitute Canard-Duchêne champagne for the Bollinger.

Mimosa: pour the orange juice into the flute and then the champagne. Stir gently. You can use sparkling white wine instead of champagne.

Black Velvet: pour 1¼ cups chilled champagne or sparkling wine and 1¼ cups chilled stout into a chilled glass at the same time. Do not stir.

Soyer au Champagne: put 1 scoop vanilla ice cream into a wine glass and add ¼ teaspoon brandy, ¼ teaspoon triple sec, and ¼ teaspoon Maraschino. Stir to mix, then top off with chilled champagne. Stir gently and decorate with a cocktail cherry.

Champagne Cup: pour ½ measure brandy and ½ measure clear Curaçao into a chilled wine glass. Add 1 ice cube and top off with champagne. Decorate with a sprig of fresh mint and a slice of orange.

Spritzer: fill a wine glass with cracked ice cubes and pour in 3 measures white wine. Top off with club soda or sparkling mineral water and decorate with a twist of lemon peel.

Did you know?

In spite of his ruthless ambition and Prussian earnestness, Otto von Bismarck must have had a more frivolous side to his nature because he is reputed to have created the Black Velvet.

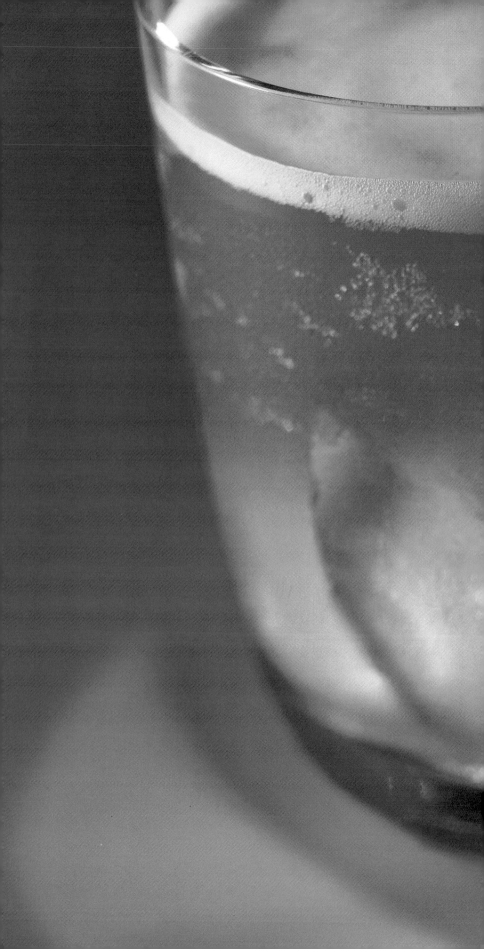

Contemporary Cocktails

Bosom Caresser

It would probably be unwise to investigate the provenance of this oddly named cocktail—perhaps it is so called because it creates a pleasantly warm glow in the cockles of the heart.

serves 1

4–6 cracked ice cubes
dash of triple sec
1 measure brandy
1 measure Madeira

❶ Put the cracked ice cubes into a mixing glass. Dash triple sec over the ice and pour in the brandy and Madeira.

❷ Stir well to mix, then strain into a chilled cocktail glass.

Rude dudes

Bosom Caresser (version 2): put 4–6 cracked ice cubes into a cocktail shaker. Pour 2 measures brandy, 1 measure Madeira, 1 measure triple sec, and 1 teaspoon grenadine over the ice, and add 1 egg yolk. Shake vigorously until a frost forms. Strain into a chilled wine glass.

Slippery Nipple: pour 2 measures white Sambuca into a chilled glass. Float 1 measure Bailey's Irish Cream on top by pouring it gently over the back of a teaspoon. Drop a dash of grenadine into the center.

Golden Nipple: put 4–6 cracked ice cubes into a cocktail shaker. Pour 1 measure Galliano and 1 measure Bailey's Irish Cream over the ice. Shake until a frost forms. Strain into a chilled cocktail glass.

Blue Movie: put 4–6 cracked ice cubes into a cocktail shaker. Pour 2 measures blue Curaçao, 1 measure vodka, 1 measure lemon juice, and 1 teaspoon sugar syrup (see page 11) over the ice. Shake vigorously until a frost forms. Strain into a chilled cocktail glass.

Did you know?

Madeira is produced in a variety of forms from Sercial and Verdelho, which are most suitable for drinking as an apéritif, to Bual and Malmsey, which are full-bodied, sweet dessert wines. Sercial is the best type to use for mixing cocktails.

Adam's Apple

Applejack in the United States, Calvados in France, and apple brandy as a generic term—whatever you call it, it provides a delicious fruity flavor and a tempting aroma to this cocktail.

serves 1

4–6 cracked ice cubes
dash of yellow Chartreuse
2 measures apple brandy
1 measure gin
1 measure dry vermouth

❶ Put the cracked ice cubes into a mixing glass. Dash the Chartreuse over the ice and pour in the apple brandy, gin, and vermouth.

❷ Stir well to mix, then strain into a chilled glass.

Garden of Eden

Eve's Apple: put 4–6 cracked ice cubes into a cocktail shaker. Pour 1 measure apple brandy, 1 measure Swedish Punsch, and 1 measure grapefruit juice. Shake vigorously until a frost forms, then strain into a chilled cocktail glass.

Eve O: put 4–6 cracked ice cubes into a mixing glass. Dash Angostura bitters over the ice and pour in 1 measure apple brandy, 1 measure gin, and ½ measure orange juice. Stir well to mix, then strain into a chilled cocktail glass.

Serpent's Tooth: put 4–6 cracked ice cubes into a cocktail shaker. Dash Angostura bitters over the ice and pour in 2 measures Irish whiskey, 1 measure sweet vermouth, 1½ measures lemon juice, and ½ measure kümmel. Shake vigorously and then pour the mixture

into a small, chilled glass. Decorate with a lemon peel twist.

Temptation: put 4–6 cracked ice cubes into a cocktail shaker. Pour 2 measures blended American whiskey, ½ measure red Dubonnet, ½ measure triple sec, and 1 teaspoon Pernod over the ice. Shake vigorously until a frost forms, then strain into a chilled cocktail glass. Decorate with a twist of lemon peel.

Bartender's Tip

Swedish Punsch is a ready-prepared aromatic sweet drink. It is usually either chilled and drunk as a liqueur or mixed with hot water and drunk as a punch, but it also features as a cocktail ingredient. It is often used in slammers and floats, such as a Broadway Smile (see page 34).

Moonraker

A powerful mix, this cocktail is more likely to fire you into orbit than to reduce you to trying to rake the moon's reflection out of a pond.

serves 1

4–6 cracked ice cubes
dash of Pernod
1 measure brandy
1 measure peach brandy
1 measure quinquina

❶ Put the cracked ice cubes into a mixing glass. Dash Pernod over the ice and pour in the brandy, peach brandy, and quinquina.

❷ Stir well to mix, then strain into a chilled highball glass.

Lunar modules

Moonshot: put 4–6 cracked ice cubes into a mixing glass. Dash Tabasco sauce over the ice and pour in 2 measures gin and 3 measures clam juice. Stir well to mix, then strain into a chilled glass.

Moon Landing: put 4–6 cracked ice cubes into a cocktail shaker. Pour 1 measure vodka, 1 measure Tia Maria, 1 measure amaretto, and 1 measure Bailey's Irish Cream over the ice. Strain into a chilled shot glass.

Moonlight: put 4–6 cracked ice cubes into a cocktail shaker. Pour 2 measures apple brandy, 2 measures lemon juice, and ½ teaspoon sugar syrup (see page 11) over the ice. Shake until a frost forms. Half fill a chilled glass with cracked ice cubes and strain the cocktail over them.

Moonrise: put 1¼ cups hard cider into a pan and add 1 tablespoon brown sugar, a pinch of ground cinnamon, and a pinch of freshly grated nutmeg. Heat gently,

stirring until the sugar has dissolved. Pour into a warmed punch glass and stir in 1 measure apple brandy. Float 2 teaspoons heavy cream on top by pouring it over the back of a teaspoon.

Moonlight Cooler: put 4–6 cracked ice cubes into a cocktail shaker. Pour 2 measures apple brandy, 1 measure lemon juice, and 1 teaspoon sugar syrup (see page 11) over the ice. Shake vigorously until a frost forms, then strain into a tall, chilled glass. Top off with sparkling water and decorate with a slice of lemon.

Bartender's Tip

Quinquina is a quinine-flavored, wine-based apéritif from France. It is not widely available but the Dubonnet company is one of the largest producers and does export its brand St. Raphael. There is no satisfactory substitute, although there are other drinks flavored with quinine.

FBR

A number of cocktails are known simply by initials. In this case, FBR stands for Frozen Brandy and Rum. Others seem to be quite obscure and, in one or two instances, slightly naughty.

serves 1

6–8 crushed ice cubes
2 measures brandy
1½ measures white rum
1 tbsp lemon juice
1 tsp sugar syrup (see page 11)
1 egg white

❶ Put the crushed ice into a blender and add the brandy, rum, lemon juice, sugar syrup, and egg white. Blend until slushy.
❷ Pour into a chilled highball glass.

Acronymic cocktails

KGB (presumably, Komityet Gosudarstvyennoi Byezopasnosti): put 4–6 cracked ice cubes into a cocktail shaker. Dash apricot brandy and lemon juice over the ice and pour in 1½ measures gin and ½ measure kümmel. Shake vigorously until a frost forms, then strain into a chilled cocktail glass.

ABM (Absolutely Bloody Marvelous): put 4–6 cracked ice cubes into a cocktail shaker. Dash Worcestershire sauce over the ice and pour in 2 measures Absolut vodka and 4 measures tomato juice. Shake vigorously until a frost forms. Half fill a chilled glass with cracked ice cubes and strain the cocktail over them.

MQS (Mary Queen of Scots): rub the rim of a chilled cocktail glass with a wedge of lemon, then dip into a saucer of superfine sugar to frost. Put 4–6 cracked ice cubes into a mixing glass. Pour 2 measures Scotch whisky, 1 measure Drambuie, and 1 measure green Chartreuse over the ice and stir to mix. Strain into the prepared glass.

BVD (Brandy, Vermouth, and Dubonnet): put 4–6 cracked ice cubes into a mixing glass. Pour 1 measure brandy, 1 measure dry vermouth, and 1 measure Dubonnet over the ice. Stir to mix and strain into a chilled cocktail glass. A modern BVD contains 1 measure white rum, 1 measure gin, and 1 measure dry vermouth.

Panda

Slivovitz is a colorless plum brandy, usually made from Mirabelle and Switzen plums. It is usually drunk straight, but can add a fruity note to cocktails. If it is not available, you could substitute apricot, peach, or cherry brandy—all fruits from the same family—but the cocktail will not look or taste quite the same.

serves 1

4-6 cracked ice cubes
dash of sugar syrup (see page 11)
1 measure slivovitz
1 measure apple brandy
1 measure gin
1 measure orange juice

❶ Put the cracked ice cubes into a cocktail shaker. Dash the sugar syrup over the ice and pour in the slivovitz, apple brandy, gin, and orange juice. Shake vigorously until a frost forms.
❷ Strain into a chilled cocktail glass.

Fruit brandy cocktails

Cadiz: put 4-6 cracked ice cubes into a cocktail shaker. Pour 1 measure blackberry brandy, 1½ measures dry sherry, ½ measure triple sec, and ½ measure light cream over the ice. Shake vigorously until a frost forms, then strain into a small, chilled glass.

Chi-Chi: half fill a chilled glass with cracked ice cubes. Pour 2 measures rum and 4 measures pineapple juice over the ice and stir to mix. Float ½ measure blackberry brandy on top by pouring it gently over the back of a teaspoon.

Vanity Fair: put 4-6 cracked ice cubes into a cocktail shaker. Pour 2 measures apple brandy, 1 measure cherry brandy, and ½ measure Maraschino over the ice. Shake vigorously until a frost forms. Strain into a chilled cocktail glass and float 1 tablespoon amaretto on top by pouring it gently over the back of a teaspoon.

Tulip: put 4-6 cracked ice cubes into a cocktail shaker. Pour 1 measure apple brandy, 1 measure sweet vermouth, ½ measure apricot brandy, and ½ measure lemon juice over the ice. Shake vigorously until a frost forms, then strain into a chilled cocktail glass.

Honeymoon

The traditional nuptial journey is so called because the first month of marriage was thought to be sweet—and why not? If you are sick of the sight of champagne following the wedding, why not share this sweet concoction?

serves 2

8–10 cracked ice cubes

4 measures apple brandy

2 measures Bénédictine

2 measures lemon juice

2 tsp triple sec

❶ Put the cracked ice cubes into a cocktail shaker. Pour the brandy, Bénédictine, lemon juice, and triple sec over the ice. Shake vigorously until a frost forms.

❷ Strain into two chilled cocktail glasses.

Wedded bliss

These cocktails all serve one.

Bachelor's Bait: put 4–6 cracked ice cubes into a cocktail shaker. Dash orange bitters over the ice, pour in 2 measures gin and 1 teaspoon grenadine, and add 1 egg white. Shake vigorously until a frost forms, then strain into a chilled cocktail glass.

Cupid: put 4–6 cracked ice cubes into a cocktail shaker. Dash Tabasco sauce over the ice, pour in 2 measures dry sherry and 1 teaspoon sugar syrup (see page 11), and add 1 egg. Shake until a frost forms, then strain into a chilled cocktail glass.

Kiss Kiss: put 4–6 cracked ice cubes into a mixing glass. Pour 1 measure cherry brandy, 1 measure gin, and 1 measure sweet vermouth over the ice. Stir well, then strain into a chilled cocktail glass.

Wedding Bells: put 4–6 cracked ice cubes into a mixing glass. Dash orange bitters over the ice and pour in 2 measures rye whiskey, 1 measure triple sec, and 2 measures Lillet. Stir well to mix, then strain into a chilled cocktail glass.

Confetti Shower: put 4–6 crushed ice cubes into a blender and add 2 measures cherry brandy, 1 measure orgeat, ¼ cup peeled, cored, and sliced apple, ½ peeled, cored, and sliced pear and ½ peeled, pitted, and sliced peach. Blend until smooth, then pour into a chilled glass.

Princess

No particular princess is specified, although a number of other cocktails are named after queens and princes, as well as princesses. Perhaps drinking this makes everyone feel like royalty.

serves 1

2 tsp chilled light cream
1 tsp superfine sugar
2 measures chilled apricot brandy

❶ Pour the cream into a small bowl and stir in the sugar.
❷ Pour the apricot brandy into a chilled liqueur glass and float the sweetened cream on top by pouring it over the back of a teaspoon.

Blue blood

Duchess: put 4–6 cracked ice cubes into a mixing glass. Pour 1 measure Pernod, 1 measure sweet vermouth, and 1 measure dry vermouth over the ice. Stir well to mix, then strain into a chilled cocktail glass.

Duke: put 4–6 cracked ice cubes into a cocktail shaker. Dash Maraschino over the ice, pour 1 measure triple sec, ¹/₂ measure lemon juice, and ¹/₂ measure orange juice over the ice, and add 1 egg white. Shake vigorously until a frost forms, then strain into a chilled wine glass. Top off with chilled champagne or sparkling wine.

Baron: put 4–6 cracked ice cubes into a mixing glass. Pour 2 measures gin, 1 measure triple sec, 1 measure dry vermouth, and 1 teaspoon sweet vermouth over the ice and stir to mix. Strain into a chilled cocktail glass.

Grand Duchess: put 4–6 cracked ice cubes into a mixing glass. Pour 2 measures vodka, 1 measure triple sec, 3 measures cranberry juice, and 2 measures orange juice over the ice. Stir well to mix. Half fill a small, chilled glass with cracked ice cubes and strain the cocktail over them.

Highland Fling

Blended whisky is best suited to cocktails—single malts should always be drunk neat or simply with a little added mineral water. However, a throat-burning, harsh blend will make a mixture closer to rocket fuel than a cocktail and no amount of additional flavors will improve it.

serves 1

4–6 cracked ice cubes

dash of Angostura bitters

2 measures Scotch whisky

1 measure sweet vermouth

cocktail olive, to decorate

❶ Put the cracked ice into a mixing glass. Dash Angostura bitters over the ice. Pour the whisky and vermouth over the ice.

❷ Stir well to mix and strain into a chilled glass. Decorate with a cocktail olive.

Variations

Beadlestone: put 4–6 cracked ice cubes into a mixing glass. Pour 2 measures Scotch whisky and 1½ measures dry vermouth over the ice. Stir well to mix, then strain into a chilled cocktail glass.

Affinity: put 4–6 cracked ice cubes into a mixing glass. Dash Angostura bitters over the ice and pour in 1 measure Scotch whisky, 1 measure dry vermouth, and 1 measure sweet vermouth. Stir well to mix, then pour into a chilled cocktail glass.

Thistle: put 4–6 cracked ice cubes into a mixing glass. Dash Angostura bitters over the ice and pour in 2 measures Scotch whisky and 1½ measures sweet vermouth. Stir and strain into a chilled cocktail glass.

Flying Scotsman: put 4–6 crushed ice cubes into a blender, dash Angostura bitters over the ice, and add 2 measures Scotch whisky, 1 measure sweet vermouth, and ¼ teaspoon sugar syrup (see page 11). Blend until slushy and pour into a small, chilled glass.

Did you know?

Angostura bitters were created by a German surgeon as a result of his work with herbal medicines in South America. His descendants still keep the secret of his formula.

Twin Peaks

Bourbon, named after a county in Kentucky, must be made from at least 51 percent corn mash and is America's most popular whiskey. It forms the basis of many more cocktails than its Scotch cousin.

serves 1

4–6 cracked ice cubes

dash of triple sec

2 measures bourbon

1 measure Bénédictine

1 measure lime juice

slice of lime, to decorate

❶ Put the cracked ice cubes into a cocktail shaker. Dash triple sec over the ice and pour in the bourbon, Bénédictine, and lime juice. Shake vigorously until a frost forms.

❷ Strain into a chilled highball glass and decorate with a slice of lime.

Variations

Confederate Railroad: put 4–6 cracked ice cubes into a cocktail shaker. Dash triple sec over the ice and pour in 2 measures bourbon, 1 measure Southern Comfort, and 1 measure orange juice. Shake vigorously until a frost forms, then strain into a chilled cocktail glass. Decorate with a slice of orange.

Queen of Memphis: put 4–6 cracked ice cubes into a cocktail shaker. Dash Maraschino over the ice and pour in 2 measures bourbon, 1 measure Midori, and 1 measure peach juice. Shake vigorously until a frost forms. Strain into a chilled cocktail glass and decorate with a wedge of melon.

Trashy Women: put 4–6 cracked ice cubes into a cocktail shaker. Dash Angostura bitters over the ice and pour in 2 measures bourbon, 1 measure Pernod, and 1 measure apple juice. Shake vigorously until a frost forms. Strain into a chilled cocktail glass and decorate with a slice of apple.

Long Gone: put 4–6 cracked ice cubes into a cocktail shaker. Dash orange bitters over the ice and pour in 2 measures bourbon, 1 measure Drambuie, and 1 measure orange juice. Shake vigorously until a frost forms, then strain into a chilled cocktail glass. Decorate with a slice of orange.

Irish Shillelagh

A shillelagh (pronounced *shee-lay-lee*) is a wooden cudgel, traditionally made from blackthorn. Undoubtedly, this is a cocktail that hits the spot.

serves 1

4–6 crushed ice cubes
2 measures Irish whiskey
1 measure lemon juice
½ measure sloe gin
½ measure white rum
½ tsp sugar syrup (see page 11)
½ peach, peeled, pitted, and finely chopped
2 raspberries, to decorate

❶ Put the crushed ice cubes into a blender and add the whiskey, lemon juice, sloe gin, rum, sugar syrup, and chopped peach. Blend until smooth.

❷ Pour into a small, chilled highball glass and decorate with raspberries.

The craic

Shillelagh: put 4–6 cracked ice cubes into a cocktail shaker. Pour 2 measures Irish whiskey, 1 measure dry sherry, 1 teaspoon golden rum, and 1 teaspoon lemon juice over the ice, and add a pinch of superfine sugar. Shake vigorously until a frost forms. Strain into a chilled cocktail glass and decorate with a cocktail cherry.

Blackthorn Bush: put 4–6 cracked ice cubes into a mixing glass. Dash Pernod and Angostura bitters over the ice and pour in 1 measure Irish whiskey and 1 measure dry vermouth. Stir well to mix, then strain into a chilled cocktail glass.

Colleen: put 4–6 cracked ice cubes into a cocktail shaker. Pour 2 measures Irish whiskey, 1 measure Irish Mist, 1 measure triple sec, and 1 teaspoon lemon juice over the ice. Shake until a frost forms, then strain into a chilled cocktail glass.

Irish Ayes: put 4–6 cracked ice cubes into a mixing glass. Pour 2 measures Irish whiskey and ½ measure green Chartreuse over the ice. Stir well to mix, then strain into a chilled cocktail glass.

Did you know?

Irish whiskey is never blended and must be matured for a minimum of five years.

Cowboy

In movies, cowboys drink their rye straight, often pulling the cork out of the bottle with their teeth, and it is certainly difficult to imagine John Wayne or Clint Eastwood sipping delicately from a chilled cocktail glass.

serves 1

4–6 cracked ice cubes
3 measures rye whiskey
2 tbsp light cream

❶ Put the cracked ice cubes into a cocktail shaker. Pour the whiskey and cream over the ice. Shake vigorously until a frost forms.
❷ Strain into a chilled highball glass.

Home on the range

Cowgirl's Prayer: half fill a tall glass with cracked ice. Pour 2 measures golden tequila and 1 measure lime juice over the ice and top off with lemonade. Stir gently to mix and decorate with slices of lemon and lime.

OK Corral: put 4–6 cracked ice cubes into a cocktail shaker. Pour 2 measures rye whiskey, 1 measure grapefruit juice, and 1 teaspoon orgeat over the ice, and shake vigorously until a frost forms. Strain into a chilled cocktail glass.

Navajo Trail: put 4–6 cracked ice cubes into a cocktail shaker. Pour 2 measures white tequila, 1 measure triple sec, 1 measure lime juice, and 1 measure cranberry juice over the ice, and shake vigorously until a frost forms. Strain into a chilled cocktail glass.

Klondike Cooler: put ½ teaspoon superfine sugar into a tall, chilled glass and add 1 measure ginger ale. Stir until the sugar has dissolved, then fill the glass with cracked ice cubes. Pour 2 measures blended American whiskey over the ice and top off with sparkling mineral water. Stir gently to mix and decorate with a spiral of lemon peel.

Cat's Eye

A cat's eye is many things—besides what a cat sees with—including a semi-precious stone and a stripy marble. Now, it's a highly potent cocktail, as pretty as a gemstone and certainly more fun than playing marbles.

serves 1

4-6 cracked ice cubes
2 measures gin
1½ measures dry vermouth
½ measure kirsch
½ measure triple sec
½ measure lemon juice
½ measure water

❶ Put the cracked ice cubes into a cocktail shaker. Pour the gin, vermouth, kirsch, triple sec, lemon juice, and water over the ice.
❷ Shake vigorously until a frost forms. Strain into a chilled goblet.

A walk on the wild side

Cheshire Cat: put 4-6 cracked ice cubes into a mixing glass. Pour 1 measure brandy, 1 measure sweet vermouth, and 1 measure orange juice over the ice. Stir well to mix, then strain into a chilled champagne flute and top off with chilled champagne. Squeeze over a twist of orange peel and decorate with an orange peel spiral.

Tiger by the Tail: put 4-6 crushed ice cubes into a blender and add 2 measures Pernod, 4 measures orange juice, and ¼ teaspoon triple sec. Blend until smooth, then pour into a chilled wine glass. Decorate with a wedge of lime.

Tiger's Milk: put 4-6 crushed ice cubes into a blender and add 2 measures golden rum, 1½ measures brandy, 1 teaspoon

sugar syrup (see page 11), and ⅔ cup milk. Blend until combined and pour into a chilled wine glass. Sprinkle with ground cinnamon.

Red Lion: put 4-6 cracked ice cubes into a cocktail shaker. Dash grenadine over the ice and pour in 2 measures Grand Marnier, 1 measure gin, 1 measure orange juice, and 1 measure lemon juice over the ice. Shake vigorously until a frost forms, then strain into a chilled cocktail glass.

White Lion: put 4-6 cracked ice cubes into a cocktail shaker. Dash Angostura bitters and grenadine over the ice and pour in 2 measures white rum, 1 measure lemon juice, and 1 teaspoon sugar syrup (see page 11). Shake vigorously until a frost forms. Strain into a chilled cocktail glass.

Road Runner

Whether it is named after the real bird or after Bugs Bunny's famous companion, this is a cocktail for slowing down after a fast-moving day, not for speeding up the pace.

serves 1

4–6 cracked ice cubes
2 measures gin
½ measure dry vermouth
½ measure Pernod
1 tsp grenadine

❶ Put the cracked ice into a cocktail shaker. Pour the gin, vermouth, Pernod, and grenadine over the ice. Shake vigorously until a frost forms.
❷ Strain into a chilled wine glass.

Variations

Road Runner (second version): put 4–6 cracked ice cubes into a cocktail shaker. Pour 1 measure vodka, ½ measure Malibu, and ½ measure amaretto over the ice, and shake vigorously until a frost forms. Strain into a chilled cocktail glass.

Fox Trot: put 4–6 cracked ice cubes into a cocktail shaker. Dash Angostura bitters over the ice and pour in 2 measures white rum and 1 teaspoon lime juice. Shake vigorously until a frost forms, then strain into a chilled cocktail glass.

Octopus's Garden: Put 4–6 cracked ice cubes into a cocktail shaker. Pour 3 measures gin and 1 measure dry vermouth over the ice. Shake vigorously until a frost forms, then strain into a chilled cocktail glass. Decorate with a black olive and a smoked baby octopus.

Elk's Own: put 4–6 cracked ice cubes into a cocktail shaker. Pour 2 measures rye whiskey, 1 measure ruby port, ½ measure lemon juice, and 1 teaspoon sugar syrup (see page 11) over the ice, and add 1 egg white. Shake vigorously until a frost forms, then strain into a chilled cocktail glass, and decorate with a pineapple wedge.

Rattlesnake: pour 1 measure chilled Bailey's Irish Cream into a shot glass. With a steady hand, gently pour in 1 measure chilled, dark crème de cacao to make a second layer, then gently pour in 1 measure chilled Kahlúa to make a third layer. Do not stir.

Shark Attack: half fill a tall, chilled glass with cracked ice cubes. Dash grenadine over the ice and pour in 3 measures vodka and 1½ measures lemonade. Stir gently.

Breakfast

It is difficult to believe that anyone would actually have the stomach to cope with cocktails first thing in the morning—but then, for those who party all night and sleep all day, cocktail time coincides with breakfast.

serves 1

4–6 cracked ice cubes

2 measures gin

1 measure grenadine

1 egg yolk

❶ Put the cracked ice cubes into a cocktail shaker. Pour the gin and grenadine over the ice and add the egg yolk. Shake vigorously until a frost forms.

❷ Strain into a chilled cocktail glass.

Mealtimes

Breakfast Egg Nog: put 4–6 cracked ice cubes into a cocktail shaker. Pour 1 measure brandy, 1 measure clear Curaçao, and 3 measures chilled milk over the ice, and add 1 egg. Shake vigorously until a frost forms, then strain into a chilled glass.

Lupy's Lunchtime Pick-me-up: put 4–6 crushed ice cubes into a blender and add 1½ measures Armagnac, 1 measure triple sec, ⅔ cup light cream, 1 teaspoon amaretto, and 1 egg. Blend until combined, then strain into a glass.

Aperitivo: put 4–6 cracked ice cubes into a mixing glass. Dash orange bitters over the ice and pour in 2 measures gin and 1½ measures white Sambuca. Stir well to mix, then strain into a chilled cocktail glass.

After Dinner: put 4–6 cracked ice cubes into a cocktail shaker. Pour 1 measure apricot brandy, 1 measure triple sec, and 1 measure lime juice over the ice. Shake vigorously until a frost forms, then strain into a chilled cocktail glass.

After Dinner (second version): put 4–6 cracked ice cubes into a cocktail shaker. Pour 1 measure cherry brandy, 1 measure prunelle liqueur, and 1 measure lemon juice over the ice. Shake vigorously until a frost forms, then strain into a chilled cocktail glass.

After Supper: put 4–6 cracked ice cubes into a cocktail shaker. Pour 1 measure apricot brandy, 1 measure triple sec, and 1 measure lemon juice over the ice. Shake vigorously until a frost forms, then strain into a chilled cocktail glass.

Suffering Bastard

You will have to make up your own mind whether this cocktail is a cure for someone already suffering or whether it is the cause of suffering still to come.

serves 1

1 tbsp Angostura bitters

6–8 cracked ice cubes

2 measures gin

1½ measures brandy

½ measure lime juice

1 tsp sugar syrup (see page 11)

ginger beer, to top off

To decorate

slice of cucumber

slice of lime

sprig of fresh mint

❶ Pour the Angostura bitters into a chilled Collins glass and swirl around, until the inside of the glass is coated. Pour out the excess and discard.

❷ Half fill the glass with cracked ice cubes. Pour the gin, brandy, lime juice, and sugar syrup over the ice. Stir well to mix.

❸ Top off with ginger beer and stir gently. Decorate with the cucumber and lime slices and a mint sprig.

Other "painful" cocktails

Ankle Breaker: put 4–6 cracked ice cubes into a cocktail shaker. Pour 2 measures dark rum, 1 measure cherry brandy, 1 measure lime juice, and 1 teaspoon sugar syrup (see page 11) over the ice. Shake until a frost forms, then strain into a small, chilled glass.

Kamikaze: put 4–6 cracked ice cubes into a cocktail shaker. Pour 3 measures vodka, ½ teaspoon lime juice, and ½ teaspoon triple sec over the ice. Shake until a frost forms, then strain into a chilled cocktail glass, and decorate with a wedge of lime.

Third Degree: put 4–6 cracked ice cubes into a mixing glass. Dash Pernod over the ice and pour in 2 measures gin and 1 measure dry vermouth. Stir well to mix, then strain into a chilled cocktail glass.

Barbed Wire: put 4–6 cracked ice cubes into a cocktail shaker. Pour 3 measures vodka, 1 teaspoon sweet vermouth, ½ teaspoon Pernod, and ½ measure dry sherry over the ice. Shake until a frost forms. Strain into a chilled cocktail glass and decorate with a twist of lemon peel.

What the Hell

Cheer yourself up when you are at a loose end, or when everything seems to have gone wrong, with this simple but delicious concoction.

serves 1

4–6 cracked ice cubes
dash of lime juice
1 measure gin
1 measure apricot brandy
1 measure dry vermouth
twist of lemon peel, to decorate

❶ Put the cracked ice cubes into a mixing glass. Dash the lime juice over the ice and pour in the gin, apricot brandy, and vermouth. Stir well to mix.

❷ Strain into a chilled glass and decorate with a twist of lemon peel.

Silly questions and answers

Why Not: put 4–6 cracked ice cubes into a mixing glass. Dash lemon juice over the ice and pour in 2 measures gin, 1 measure peach brandy, and 1 measure Noilly Prat. Stir to mix. Strain into a chilled glass.

Is This All: put 4–6 cracked ice cubes into a cocktail shaker. Pour 2 measures lemon vodka, 1 measure triple sec, and 1 measure lemon juice over the ice, and add 1 egg white. Shake until a frost forms, then strain into a chilled cocktail glass.

What The Dickens: pour 2 measures gin into a heatproof glass and stir in 1½ teaspoons confectioners' sugar. Top off with hot water.

This Is It: put 4–6 cracked ice cubes into a cocktail shaker. Pour 2 measures gin, 1 measure triple sec, and 1 measure lemon juice over the ice, and then add 1 egg white. Shake vigorously until a frost forms, then strain the mixture into a chilled cocktail glass.

Did you know?

French vermouth, of which Noilly Prat is the leading brand, is almost always dry, whereas sweet red vermouth is still the most popular type in Italy, although all the well-known brands—Martini, Cinzano, and Gancia—also include a dry version. Each firm keeps its own formula secret.

Nirvana

It may not be possible to obtain a perfect state of harmony and bliss through a cocktail, but this has to be the next best thing.

serves 1

8–10 cracked ice cubes
2 measures dark rum
½ measure grenadine
½ measure tamarind syrup
1 tsp sugar syrup (see page 11)
grapefruit juice, to top off

❶ Put 4–6 cracked ice cubes into a cocktail shaker. Pour the rum, grenadine, tamarind syrup, and sugar syrup over the ice and shake vigorously until a frost forms.
❷ Half fill a chilled Collins glass with cracked ice cubes and strain the cocktail over them. Top off with grapefruit juice.

Heavenly bliss

Paradise: put 4–6 cracked ice cubes into a cocktail shaker. Pour 2 measures apricot brandy, 1 measure gin, 1½ measures orange juice, and ½ teaspoon grenadine over the ice. Shake vigorously until a frost forms. Strain into a chilled cocktail glass.

Heavenly: put 4–6 cracked ice cubes into a mixing glass. Pour 1½ measures brandy, ½ measure cherry brandy, and ½ measure plum brandy over the ice, and stir well to mix. Strain into a chilled cocktail glass.

Seventh Heaven: put 4–6 cracked ice cubes into a cocktail shaker. Pour 2 measures gin, ½ measure Maraschino, and ½ measure grapefruit juice over the ice. Shake vigorously until a frost forms, then strain into a chilled cocktail glass. Decorate with a sprig of fresh mint.

Ambrosia: put 4–6 cracked ice cubes into a cocktail shaker. Pour 1½ measures brandy, 1½ measures apple brandy, and ½ teaspoon raspberry syrup over the ice. Shake vigorously until a frost forms and strain into a chilled wine glass. Top off with chilled champagne and decorate with a raspberry.

Frozen Daiquiri

One of the great classic cocktails, the Daiquiri (see page 70) has moved on. It's not just mixed with fresh fruit or unusual ingredients, it's entered the twenty-first century with a whole new future, as slushes take on a leading role in fashionable cocktail bars.

serves 1

6 crushed ice cubes

2 measures white rum

1 measure lime juice

1 tsp sugar syrup (see page 11)

slice of lime, to decorate

❶ Put the crushed ice into a blender and add the rum, lime juice, and sugar syrup. Blend until slushy.

❷ Pour into a chilled champagne flute and decorate with the lime slice.

Variations

Frozen Pineapple Daiquiri: put 6 crushed ice cubes into a blender and add 2 measures white rum, 1 measure lime juice, ½ teaspoon pineapple syrup, and ½ cup finely chopped fresh pineapple. Blend until slushy, then pour into a chilled cocktail glass. Decorate with pineapple wedges.

Frozen Mint Daiquiri: put 6 crushed ice cubes into a blender and add 2 measures white rum, ½ measure lime juice, 1 teaspoon sugar syrup (see page 11), and 6 fresh mint leaves. Blend until slushy, then pour into a chilled cocktail glass.

Frozen Strawberry Daiquiri: put 6 crushed ice cubes into a blender and add 2 measures white rum, 1 measure lime juice, 1 teaspoon sugar syrup (see page 11), and 6 fresh or frozen strawberries. Blend until slushy, then pour into a chilled glass. Decorate with a strawberry.

Frozen Peach Daiquiri: put 6 crushed ice cubes into a blender. Add 2 measures white rum, 1 measure lime juice, 1 teaspoon sugar syrup (see page 11), and ½ peeled, pitted, and finely chopped peach. Blend until slushy, then pour into a chilled cocktail glass. Decorate with a peach slice.

Talk To Tom !

GREEN MOUNTAINS REALTOR .

Metro Brokers - Tom Evon Realty · Office: 303-987-0404
Fax: 303-987-0427 E-mail: talk2tom@realtor.com
355 Union Blvd #10 Lakewood, Co. 80228

If you prefer not to receive these pads, leave a message
with your address to be removed from the delivery list.

Cinderella

If the fairy-story heroine had been knocking back cocktails until the clock struck midnight, it's hardly surprising that she forgot the time, mislaid her pumpkin, and lost her shoe on the way home.

serves 1

4-6 cracked ice cubes
3 measures white rum
1 measure white port
1 measure lemon juice
1 tsp sugar syrup (see page 11)
1 egg white

❶ Put the cracked ice cubes into a cocktail shaker. Pour the rum, port, lemon juice, and sugar syrup over the ice and add the egg white.
❷ Shake vigorously until a frost forms and strain into a chilled glass.

And they all lived happily ever after

Glass Slipper: put 4-6 cracked ice cubes into a cocktail shaker. Pour 3 measures gin and 1 measure blue Curaçao over the ice. Shake vigorously until a frost forms, then strain into a chilled cocktail glass.

Prince Charming: put 4-6 cracked ice cubes into a cocktail shaker. Pour 2 measures vodka, 1 measure apricot brandy, 1 measure apple brandy, and 1 teaspoon lemon juice over the ice. Shake vigorously until a frost forms, then strain into a chilled cocktail glass.

Peter Pan: put 4-6 cracked ice cubes into a cocktail shaker. Pour 1 measure gin, 1 measure dry vermouth, 1 measure peach brandy, and 1 measure orange juice over the ice. Shake until a frost forms, then strain into a chilled cocktail glass.

Tinkerbell: put 4-6 cracked ice cubes into a cocktail shaker. Dash grenadine over the ice, pour in 2 measures vodka and 1 measure cherry brandy, and add 1 egg white. Shake vigorously until a frost forms, then strain into a chilled cocktail glass.

Did you know?

White port is made from green grapes and when it was originally produced, it was invariably sweet and heavy. It has undergone a complete change of style and nowadays, it is dry and light.

Josiah's Bay Float

This is a wonderful cocktail for a special occasion in the summer. Since it is made for two to share, perhaps an engagement party or a romantic *al fresco* dinner would be appropriate. For the more prosaic, serve it in two tall, chilled glasses rather than a pineapple shell.

serves 2

8–10 cracked ice cubes

2 measures golden rum

1 measure Galliano

2 measures pineapple juice

1 measure lime juice

4 tsp sugar syrup (see page 11)

champagne, to top off

To decorate

slices of lime

slices of lemon

cocktail cherries

To serve

scooped-out pineapple shell

❶ Put the ice cubes into a cocktail shaker. Pour the rum, Galliano, pineapple juice, lime juice, and sugar syrup over the ice. Shake vigorously until a frost forms.

❷ Strain into the pineapple shell, top off with champagne, and stir gently. Decorate with lime and lemon slices and cocktail cherries and serve with two straws.

Variation

Royal Matador (for two): cut off the top of a pineapple and reserve the "lid." Scoop out the flesh, leaving the shell intact. Put the flesh in a blender and purée. Strain the juice from the purée and return it to the blender. Add 8–10 crushed ice cubes, 4 measures golden tequila, 1½ measures crème de framboise, 2 measures lime juice, and 1 tablespoon amaretto. Blend until slushy, then pour into the pineapple shell, adding more ice if required. Replace the "lid" and serve with straws.

Palm Beach

If it's been a long time since your last vacation, conjure up the blue skies of Florida and the rolling surf with this sunny cocktail.

serves 1

4–6 cracked ice cubes
1 measure white rum
1 measure gin
1 measure pineapple juice

❶ Put the cracked ice into a cocktail shaker. Pour the rum, gin, and pineapple juice over the ice. Shake vigorously until a frost forms.

❷ Strain into a chilled highball glass.

Taking time out

Miami Beach: put 4–6 cracked ice cubes into a cocktail shaker. Pour 2 measures Scotch whisky, 1½ measures dry vermouth, and 2 measures grapefruit juice over the ice. Shake vigorously until a frost forms, then strain into a chilled cocktail glass.

Florida: put 4–6 cracked ice cubes into a cocktail shaker. Pour 1 measure gin, 1 teaspoon triple sec, 1 teaspoon kirsch, and 2 measures orange juice over the ice. Shake vigorously until a frost forms, then strain into a chilled cocktail glass.

Grand Bahama: put 4–6 cracked ice cubes into a cocktail shaker. Pour 1 measure white rum, ½ measure brandy, ½ measure triple sec, and 1 measure lime juice over the ice. Shake vigorously until a frost forms, then strain into a chilled cocktail glass.

Bermuda Bloom: put 4–6 cracked ice cubes into a cocktail shaker. Dash triple sec over the ice and pour in 1 measure gin, 1 measure lemon juice, 1 measure orange juice, ½ measure apricot brandy, and 1 teaspoon sugar syrup (see page 11). Shake vigorously until a frost forms, then strain into a chilled cocktail glass.

Deauville: put 4–6 cracked ice cubes into a cocktail shaker. Pour 1½ measures brandy, 1 measure apple brandy, ½ measure triple sec, and ½ measure lemon juice over the ice. Shake vigorously until a frost forms, then strain into a chilled glass.

Costa del Sol: put 4–6 cracked ice cubes into a cocktail shaker. Pour 2 measures gin, 1 measure apricot brandy, and 1 measure triple sec over the ice. Shake vigorously until a frost forms, then strain into a chilled cocktail glass.

Hayden's Milk Float

An irresistible melding of perfect partners—rum, cherry, chocolate, and cream—this cocktail is almost too good to be true.

serves 1

4–6 cracked ice cubes
2 measures white rum
1 measure kirsch
1 measure white crème de cacao
1 measure light cream

To decorate
grated chocolate
cocktail cherry

❶ Put the cracked ice cubes into a cocktail shaker. Pour the rum, kirsch, crème de cacao, and cream over the ice. Shake vigorously until a frost forms.
❷ Strain into a chilled highball glass. Sprinkle with grated chocolate and decorate with a cocktail cherry.

From the dairy

Bourbon Milk Punch: put 4–6 cracked ice cubes into a cocktail shaker. Dash vanilla extract over the ice and pour in 2 measures bourbon, 3 measures milk, and 1 teaspoon clear honey. Shake vigorously until a frost forms. Strain into a small, chilled glass and sprinkle with freshly grated nutmeg.

Irish Cow: heat 1 cup milk in a small pan to just below boiling point. Remove from the heat and pour into a warmed punch glass or mug. Pour in 2 measures Irish whiskey and 1 teaspoon superfine sugar. Stir until the sugar has dissolved.

Brown Cow: put 4–6 cracked ice cubes into a cocktail shaker. Pour 1 measure Kahlúa and 3 measures chilled milk over the ice. Shake vigorously until a frost forms. Half fill a small, chilled glass with cracked ice cubes and strain the cocktail over them.

Egg Nog (to serve 24): separate 12 eggs and place the yolks in a punch bowl, reserving the whites. Add 1 cup superfine sugar to the yolks and beat well. Whip 2½ cups heavy cream and then stir it into the egg yolk mixture with 3 cups milk. Stir in 3 cups brandy, cover with plastic wrap, and chill in the refrigerator for 1½ hours. Put the egg whites in a separate bowl, cover with plastic wrap, and then chill in the refrigerator for 1½ hours. Just before serving, whisk the egg whites until stiff, then fold them into the brandy mixture. Sprinkle with freshly grated nutmeg.

Bishop

It is strange how men of the cloth have gained a reputation for being enthusiastic about the good, material things in life. Even Rudyard Kipling wrote about smuggling "brandy for the parson." It goes to show that spirituality is no barrier to spirits.

serves 1

4–6 cracked ice cubes

2 dashes of lemon juice

2 measures white rum

1 tbsp red wine

pinch of caster sugar

❶ Put the cracked ice cubes into a cocktail shaker. Dash the lemon juice over the ice, pour in the white rum and red wine, and add a pinch of sugar. Shake vigorously until a frost forms.

❷ Strain into a chilled wine glass.

Interdenominational cocktails

Piscy Bishop: put 4–6 cracked ice cubes into a cocktail shaker. Pour 2 measures Scotch whisky, 1 measure dry vermouth, 1 teaspoon triple sec, and 1 teaspoon orange juice over the ice, and add a pinch of superfine sugar. Shake vigorously until a frost forms. Strain into a chilled cocktail glass.

Presbyterian: half fill a glass with cracked ice cubes. Pour 3 measures bourbon, 3 measures ginger ale, and 3 measures sparkling mineral water over the ice. Stir gently.

Parish Priest: put 4–6 cracked ice cubes into a cocktail shaker. Dash triple sec, Pernod, and orange bitters over the ice, and pour in 2 measures Irish whiskey and 1 measure sweet vermouth. Shake vigorously until a frost forms, then strain into a chilled cocktail glass.

Curate's Egg: put 4–6 crushed ice cubes into a blender and add 2 measures brandy, 1 measure Tia Maria, 1 measure sweet sherry, ¾ cup light cream, 1 teaspoon sugar syrup (see page 11), and 1 egg. Blend until smooth, then pour into a tall, chilled glass.

Quaker's: put 4–6 cracked ice cubes into a cocktail shaker. Pour 1 measure brandy, 1 measure white rum, ½ measure lemon juice, and ½ measure raspberry syrup over the ice. Shake vigorously until a frost forms, then strain into a chilled cocktail glass.

Puritan: put 4–6 cracked ice cubes into a cocktail shaker. Dash apricot brandy and orange juice over the ice and pour in 1 measure gin and 1 measure Lillet. Shake vigorously until a frost forms, then strain into a chilled cocktail glass.

El Diablo

One or two Diablos and you will certainly feel a bit of a devil, but one or two too many and you will feel like the very devil!

serves 1

6–8 cracked ice cubes
2–3 strips of lime peel
1 measure lime juice
3 measures white tequila
1 measure crème de cassis

❶ Fill a small, chilled glass with cracked ice cubes and add the lime peel.

❷ Pour the lime juice over the ice and add the tequila and crème de cassis.

Devilish drinks

Diablo: put 4–6 cracked ice cubes into a cocktail shaker. Dash lemon juice over the ice and pour in 2 measures white port and 1 measure dry vermouth. Shake until a frost forms. Strain into a chilled glass and decorate with a lemon peel twist.

Devil's Cocktail: put 4–6 cracked ice cubes into a mixing glass. Dash lemon juice over the ice and pour in 2 measures ruby port and 1 measure dry vermouth. Stir well. Strain the mixture into a chilled cocktail glass. Decorate with a lemon peel twist.

Black Devil: put 4–6 cracked ice cubes into a mixing glass. Pour 2 measures white rum and ½ measure dry vermouth over the ice and then stir well to mix. Strain into a chilled cocktail glass and decorate with a pitted black olive.

Blue Devil: put 4–6 cracked ice cubes into a cocktail shaker. Pour 2 measures gin, ½ measure lime juice, 1 tablespoon Maraschino, and 1 teaspoon blue Curaçao over the ice. Shake until a frost forms. Strain into a chilled cocktail glass.

Did you know?

Tequila is a secondary product of the agave plant, which was originally used to produce pulque, a fermented, milky liquor. Pulque is reputed to taste quite disgusting and, although it was popular with native Mexicans, Spanish colonists preferred to distil it to produce tequila.

Huatusco Whammer

To be authentic, this cocktail should be topped off with Coca-Cola, but you can use other brands of cola if you prefer. Make sure that the cola is well chilled before adding it.

serves 1

8–10 cracked ice cubes
1 measure white tequila
½ measure white rum
½ measure vodka
½ measure gin
½ measure triple sec
1 measure lemon juice
½ tsp sugar syrup (see page 11)
cola, to top off

❶ Put 4–6 cracked ice cubes into a cocktail shaker. Pour the tequila, rum, vodka, gin, triple sec, lemon juice, and sugar syrup over the ice. Shake vigorously until a frost forms.

❷ Fill a chilled Collins glass with cracked ice cubes and strain the cocktail over them. Top off with cola, stir gently, and serve with straws.

Variations

Mexicola: half fill a tall, chilled glass with cracked ice cubes. Pour 2 measures tequila and 1 measure lime juice over the ice and top off with cola. Stir gently and decorate with a slice of lime.

Cherrycola: half fill a tall, chilled glass with cracked ice. Pour 2 measures cherry brandy and 1 measure lemon juice over the ice. Top off with cola, stir gently, and decorate with a slice of lemon.

Lounge Lizard: half fill a tall, chilled glass with cracked ice cubes. Add 2 measures dark rum and 1 measure amaretto. Top off with cola and stir.

Coco Loco

This is a truly spectacular cocktail and can be great fun to decorate. Look out for swizzle sticks in the shape of palm trees or hula dancers and elaborately curly straws.

serves 1

1 fresh coconut
8–10 crushed ice cubes
2 measures white tequila
1 measure gin
1 measure white rum
2 measures pineapple juice
1 tsp sugar syrup (see page 11)
½ lime

❶ Carefully saw the top off the coconut, reserving the liquid inside.

❷ Add the crushed ice, tequila, gin, rum, pineapple juice, and sugar syrup to the coconut, together with the reserved coconut liquid.

❸ Squeeze the lime over the cocktail and drop it in. Stir well and serve with a straw.

Coconut shy

Coconut Tequila: put 4–6 cracked ice cubes into a cocktail shaker. Dash lemon juice and Maraschino over the ice and pour in 1 measure white tequila and ½ measure Malibu. Shake vigorously until a frost forms, then strain into a chilled cocktail glass.

Blue Hawaiian: put 4–6 cracked ice cubes into a cocktail shaker. Pour in 1 measure white rum, 1 measure blue Curaçao, 1 measure Malibu, and 2 measures pineapple juice. Shake vigorously until a frost forms. Half fill a chilled glass with cracked ice cubes and strain the cocktail over them. Decorate with a cocktail cherry.

Beautiful Beth: put 4–6 cracked ice cubes into a cocktail shaker. Pour 2 measures white rum, 1 measure Malibu, and ½ measure triple sec over the ice. Shake vigorously until a frost forms. Half fill a chilled glass with cracked ice cubes and then strain the cocktail over them. Top off with cola and decorate with some cocktail cherries.

Coconut Daiquiri: put 4–6 crushed ice cubes into a cocktail shaker. Pour 2 measures white rum, 1 measure Malibu, 2 measures lime juice, and 1 measure grenadine over the ice, and shake until a frost forms. Strain into a chilled cocktail glass and decorate with a slice of lime.

Tequila Mockingbird

In spite of the horrible literary pun in the name, this popular cocktail is fast becoming a modern classic.

serves 1

4–6 cracked ice cubes
2 measures white tequila
1 measure white crème de menthe
1 measure fresh lime juice

❶ Put the cracked ice cubes into a cocktail shaker. Add the tequila, crème de menthe, and lime juice. Shake vigorously until a frost forms.

❷ Strain into a chilled highball glass.

Strictly for the birds

Bird of Paradise: put 4–6 cracked ice cubes into a cocktail shaker. Pour 1½ measures white tequila, ½ measure white crème de cacao, ½ measure Galliano, 1 measure orange juice, and ½ measure light cream over the ice. Shake vigorously until a frost forms, then strain into a chilled wine glass.

Bird of Paradise Cooler: put 4–6 cracked ice cubes into a cocktail shaker. Pour 2 measures gin, 1 measure lemon juice, 1 teaspoon grenadine, and 1 teaspoon sugar syrup (see page 11) over the ice, and add 1 egg white. Shake vigorously until a frost forms. Half fill a chilled glass with cracked ice cubes and pour the cocktail over them. Top off with sparkling mineral water.

Blue Bird: put 4–6 cracked ice cubes into a cocktail shaker. Dash Angostura bitters over the ice and pour in 3 measures gin and 1 measure blue Curaçao. Shake vigorously until a frost forms, then strain into a chilled cocktail glass.

Did you know?

Crème de menthe, just about the only liqueur flavored with a single herb rather than a mixture, was always colored green when it was first produced. Nowadays, white crème de menthe, which is no different in flavor, is widely available.

Tequila Slammer

Slammers, also known as shooters, are currently very fashionable. The idea is that you pour the different ingredients directly into the glass, without stirring (some slammers form colorful layers). Cover the top of the glass with one hand to prevent spillage, then slam the glass on the bar or a table to mix, and drink the cocktail down in one. It is essential to use a strong glass that is unlikely to break under such treatment.

serves 1

1 measure white tequila
1 measure lemon juice
chilled sparkling wine, to top off

❶ Put the tequila and lemon juice into a chilled glass and stir to mix. Top off with sparkling wine.
❷ Cover the glass with your hand and slam.

"Those little shooters, how I love to drink them down..."

Alabama Slammer: put 4–6 cracked ice cubes into a mixing glass. Pour 1 measure Southern Comfort, 1 measure amaretto, and ½ measure sloe gin over the ice and stir to mix. Strain into a shot glass and add ½ teaspoon lemon juice. Cover and slam.

B52: pour 1 measure chilled dark crème de cacao into a shot glass. With a steady hand, gently pour in 1 measure chilled Bailey's Irish Cream to make a second layer, then gently pour in 1 measure chilled Grand Marnier. Cover and slam.

B52 (second version): pour 1 measure chilled Kahlúa into a shot glass. With a steady hand, gently pour in 1 measure chilled Bailey's Irish Cream to make a second layer, then gently pour in 1 measure chilled Grand Marnier. Cover and slam.

Banana Slip: pour 1 measure chilled crème de banane into a shot glass. With a steady hand, gently pour in 1 measure chilled Bailey's Irish Cream to make a second layer. Cover and slam.

Wild Night Out

Tequila has a reputation for being an extraordinarily potent spirit, but most commercially exported brands are the same standard strength as other spirits, such as gin or whiskey. "Home-grown" tequila or its close relative, *mescal*, may be another matter.

serves 1

4–6 cracked ice cubes
3 measures white tequila
2 measures cranberry juice
1 measure lime juice
club soda, to top off

❶ Put the cracked ice cubes into a cocktail shaker. Pour the tequila, cranberry juice, and lime juice over the ice. Shake vigorously until a frost forms.
❷ Half fill a chilled highball glass with cracked ice cubes and strain the cocktail over them. Add club soda to taste.

The wild bunch

Buttafuoco: put 4–6 cracked ice cubes into a cocktail shaker. Pour 2 measures white tequila, ½ measure Galliano, ½ measure cherry brandy, and ½ measure lemon juice over the ice. Shake vigorously until a frost forms. Half fill a glass with cracked ice cubes and strain the cocktail over them. Top off with club soda and decorate with a cocktail cherry.

Magna Carta: rub the rim of a wine glass with a wedge of lime, then dip in a saucer of superfine sugar to frost. Put 4–6 cracked ice cubes into a mixing glass. Pour 2 measures white tequila and 1 measure triple sec over the ice and stir well to mix.

Strain into the prepared glass and top off with chilled sparkling wine.

Tequila Fizz: put 4–6 cracked ice cubes into a cocktail shaker. Pour 3 measures white tequila, 1 measure grenadine, and 1 measure lime juice over the ice and add 1 egg white. Shake vigorously until a frost forms. Half fill a chilled glass with cracked ice cubes and strain the cocktail over them. Top off with ginger ale.

Changuirongo: half fill a tall, chilled glass with cracked ice cubes. Pour 2 measures white tequila over the ice and top off with ginger ale. Stir gently and decorate with a slice of lime.

Carolina

White tequila is most commonly used for mixing cocktails, but some require the mellower flavor of the amber-colored, aged tequilas, which are known as golden tequila or *añejo*.

serves 1

4–6 cracked ice cubes
3 measures golden tequila
1 tsp grenadine
1 tsp vanilla extract
1 measure light cream
1 egg white

To decorate
ground cinnamon
cocktail cherry

❶ Put the cracked ice cubes into a cocktail shaker. Pour the tequila, grenadine, vanilla, and cream over the ice and add the egg white. Shake vigorously until a frost forms.

❷ Strain into a chilled cocktail glass. Sprinkle with cinnamon and decorate with a cocktail cherry.

The golden touch

Grapeshot: put 4–6 cracked ice cubes into a cocktail shaker. Pour 2 measures golden tequila, 1 measure clear Curaçao, and 1½ measures white grape juice over the ice and shake vigorously until a frost forms. Strain into a chilled cocktail glass.

Chapala: put 4–6 cracked ice cubes into a cocktail shaker. Pour 2 measures golden tequila, 2 measures orange juice, 1 measure lime juice, ½ measure triple sec, and ½ measure grenadine over the ice. Shake vigorously until a frost forms. Half fill a

chilled glass with cracked ice cubes and strain the cocktail over them.

Piñata: put 4–6 cracked ice cubes into a cocktail shaker and add 2 measures golden tequila, 1 measure crème de banane, and 1½ measures lime juice. Shake until a frost forms. Strain into a chilled glass.

Montezuma: put 4–6 crushed ice cubes into a blender and add 2 measures golden tequila, 1 measure Madeira, and 1 egg yolk. Blend until smooth, then pour into a chilled cocktail glass.

Chili Willy

Truly a cocktail for the brave-hearted—the heat depends on the type of chili, since some are much more fiery than others, as well as the quantity you add and whether the chili was seeded first. For an even spicier cocktail, use chili vodka instead of plain.

serves 1

4–6 cracked ice cubes
2 measures vodka
1 tsp chopped fresh chili

❶ Put the ice into a cocktail shaker. Pour the vodka over the ice and add the chile.
❷ Shake until a frost forms and strain into a chilled glass.

Flavored vodkas

Kuch Behar: put 6–8 cracked ice cubes into a chilled glass. Pour 1 measure pepper vodka and 1 measure tomato juice over the ice. Stir well to mix.

Hot and Dirty Martini: put 4–6 cracked ice cubes into a cocktail shaker. Pour 3 measures pepper vodka, ½ measure dry vermouth, and 1 teaspoon olive brine over the ice. Shake until a frost forms. Strain into a chilled cocktail glass. Decorate with a stuffed olive. (For a Martini and other variations, see page 40.)

Fuzzy Martini: put 4–6 cracked ice cubes into a cocktail shaker. Pour 2 measures vanilla vodka, ½ measure coffee vodka, and 1 teaspoon peach schnapps over the ice. Shake until a frost forms. Strain into a chilled cocktail glass and decorate with a slice of peach.

Stockholm: put a sugar lump in a goblet and add 2 measures lemon vodka, and 1 measure lemon juice. Stir until thoroughly dissolved. Top off with chilled sparkling wine.

Did you know?

It is a popular misconception that the heat of a chili is in the seeds. In fact, they contain no capsaicin—the heat factor—at all; the heat is most concentrated in the flesh immediately surrounding them. Seeding the chilies removes most of this intensely hot flesh.

Crocodile

This is certainly a snappy cocktail with a bit of bite. However, it probably gets its name from its spectacular color—Midori, a Japanese melon-flavored liqueur, which is a startling shade of green.

serves 1

4–6 cracked ice cubes

2 measures vodka

1 measure triple sec

1 measure Midori

2 measures lemon juice

❶ Put the cracked ice cubes into a cocktail shaker. Pour the vodka, triple sec, Midori, and lemon juice over the ice. Shake vigorously until a frost forms.

❷ Strain into a chilled cocktail glass.

Variations

Alligator: put 4–6 cracked ice cubes into a cocktail shaker. Pour 2 measures vodka, 1 measure Midori, ½ measure dry vermouth, and ¼ teaspoon lemon juice over the ice. Shake vigorously until a frost forms. Strain into a chilled cocktail glass.

Melon Ball: put 4–6 cracked ice cubes into a mixing glass. Pour 2 measures vodka, 2 measures Midori, and 4 measures pineapple juice over the ice and stir well to mix. Half fill a chilled glass with cracked ice cubes and strain the cocktail over them. Decorate with a melon wedge.

Melon Balls: put 4–6 cracked ice cubes into a cocktail shaker. Pour 1 measure vodka, 1 measure Midori, and 1 measure pineapple juice over the ice. Shake vigorously until a frost forms, then strain into a chilled cocktail glass.

Melon State Balls: put 4–6 cracked ice cubes into a cocktail shaker. Pour 2 measures vodka, 1 measure Midori, and 2 measures orange juice over the ice. Shake vigorously until a frost forms, then strain the mixture into a chilled cocktail glass.

Grimace and Grin

Cocktails flavored with candies are very fashionable, which is probably indicative of how enthusiastically a new, young generation is rediscovering the joys of mixed drinks.

serves 15-20

³/₄ cup sharp-flavored
jellybeans, such as sour cherry,
lemon, and apple
³/₄ bottle vodka, about
2¼ cups

❶ Reserve ¼ cup of the jellybeans and place the remainder in a microwave-proof or heatproof bowl. Add about 4 tablespoons of the vodka. Either microwave until the jellybeans have melted or set the bowl over a pan of barely simmering water and heat until the beans have melted.

❷ Pour the mixture through a funnel into the vodka remaining in the bottle and add the reserved jellybeans. Replace the cap and chill in the refrigerator for at least 2 hours.

❸ To serve, shake the bottle vigorously, then pour into chilled glasses.

Confectionery concoctions

Gumdrop Martini: rub the rim of a chilled cocktail glass with a wedge of lemon, then dip in a saucer of superfine sugar to frost. Put 4–6 cracked ice cubes into a cocktail shaker. Pour 2 measures lemon rum, 1 measure vodka, ½ measure Southern Comfort, ½ measure lemon juice, and ½ teaspoon dry vermouth over the ice. Shake vigorously until a frost forms, then strain into the prepared glass. Decorate with gumdrops.

Good and Plenty: put 1 measure vodka, 1 measure Kahlúa, a dash of Pernod, and

1 scoop vanilla ice cream into a blender. Blend until combined, then pour into a chilled wine glass.

London Fog: put 1 measure white crème de menthe, 1 measure Pernod, and 1 scoop vanilla ice cream into a blender. Blend until combined and pour into a small chilled glass.

One Ireland: pour 2 measures Irish whiskey, 1 measure green crème de menthe, and 1 scoop vanilla ice cream into a blender. Blend until smooth, then pour into a chilled cocktail glass.

Polynesian Pepper Pot

It may seem strange to make a sweet drink and then season it with pepper and spices, but there is a long and honorable culinary tradition of making the most of the slightly acerbic flavor of pineapple in this kind of way.

serves 1

4–6 cracked ice cubes

dash of Tabasco sauce

2 measures vodka

1 measure golden rum

4 measures pineapple juice

½ measure orgeat

1 tsp lemon juice

¼ tsp cayenne pepper

pinch of curry powder, to decorate

❶ Put the cracked ice into a cocktail shaker. Dash Tabasco sauce over the ice, pour in the vodka, rum, pineapple juice, orgeat, and lemon juice and add the cayenne. Shake vigorously until a frost forms.

❷ Strain into a chilled glass and sprinkle curry powder on top.

Totally tropical

Polynesian Sour: put 4–6 crushed ice cubes into a blender and add 2 measures light rum, ½ measure guava juice, ½ measure lemon juice, and ½ measure orange juice. Blend the mixture until smooth, then pour into a chilled cocktail glass.

Polynesia: put 4–6 cracked ice cubes into a cocktail shaker. Dash Angostura bitters over the ice and add 2 measures white rum, 2 measures passion fruit juice, 1 measure lime juice, and 1 egg white. Shake vigorously until a frost forms, then strain into a chilled cocktail glass.

Did you know?

Tabasco sauce was invented in New Orleans in the middle of the nineteenth century. It is a hot chili sauce, which is matured in oak barrels for several years. Originally it was made from red chilies and this is still the most popular variety, but a green version is now also available.

Fuzzy Navel

This is another one of those cocktails with a name that plays on the ingredients—fuzzy to remind you that it contains peach schnapps and navel because it is mixed with orange juice. It is no reflection on anyone's personal hygiene.

serves 1

4–6 cracked ice cubes
2 measures vodka
1 measure peach schnapps
1 cup orange juice
slice of orange, to decorate

❶ Put the cracked ice cubes into a cocktail shaker. Pour the vodka, peach schnapps, and orange juice over the ice. Shake vigorously until a frost forms.
❷ Strain into a chilled glass and decorate with a slice of orange.

Variations

Halley's Comfort: half fill a tall, chilled glass with cracked ice cubes. Pour 2 measures Southern Comfort and 2 measures peach schnapps over the ice and top off with sparkling mineral water. Stir and decorate with a slice of lemon.

Woo-woo: half fill a chilled glass with cracked ice. Pour 2 measures vodka, 2 measures peach schnapps and 4 measures cranberry juice over the ice. Stir well.

Royal Wedding: put 4–6 cracked ice cubes into a cocktail shaker. Pour 1 measure kirsch, 1 measure peach brandy, and 1 measure orange juice over the ice. Shake vigorously until a frost forms, then strain into a chilled cocktail glass.

Southern Peach: put 4–6 cracked ice cubes into a cocktail shaker. Dash Angostura bitters over the ice and pour in 1 measure Southern Comfort, 1 measure peach brandy, and 1 measure light cream. Shake vigorously until a frost forms, then strain into a chilled cocktail glass. Decorate with a slice of peach.

Vodga

As a rule, classic cocktails based on vodka were intended to provide the kick of an alcoholic drink with no tell-tale signs on the breath and they were usually fairly simple mixes of fruit juice, sodas, and other nonalcoholic flavorings. By contrast, contemporary cocktails based on vodka often include other aromatic and flavorsome spirits and liqueurs, with vodka adding extra strength.

serves 1

4-6 cracked ice cubes
2 measures vodka
1 measure Strega
½ measure orange juice

❶ Put the cracked ice cubes into a cocktail shaker. Pour the vodka, Strega, and orange juice over the ice. Shake vigorously until a frost forms.
❷ Strain into a chilled cocktail glass.

Variations

Golden Frog: put 4-6 crushed ice cubes into a blender and add 1 measure vodka, 1 measure Strega, 1 measure Galliano, and 1 measure lemon juice. Blend until slushy, then pour into a chilled cocktail glass.

Genoese: put 4-6 cracked ice cubes into a cocktail shaker. Pour 1 measure vodka, 1 measure grappa, ½ measure Sambuca, and ½ measure dry vermouth over the ice. Shake vigorously until a frost forms, then strain into a chilled cocktail glass.

White Spider: put 4-6 cracked ice cubes into a mixing glass. Pour 1 measure vodka and 1 measure white crème de menthe over the ice. Stir well to mix, then strain into a chilled cocktail glass.

Tailgate: put 4-6 cracked ice cubes into a mixing glass. Dash orange bitters over the ice and pour in 2 measures vodka, 1 measure green Chartreuse, and 1 measure sweet vermouth. Stir well to mix, then strain into a chilled cocktail glass.

Mudslide

This ominous-sounding cocktail is actually a gorgeously creamy and richly-flavored concoction that is delicious whatever the weather conditions.

serves 1

4–6 cracked ice cubes
1½ measures Kahlúa
1½ measures Bailey's Irish Cream
1½ measures vodka

❶ Put the cracked ice cubes into a cocktail shaker. Pour the Kahlúa, Bailey's Irish Cream, and vodka over the ice. Shake vigorously until a frost forms.
❷ Strain into a chilled goblet.

Meteorological mixes

Dark and Stormy: half fill a chilled glass with cracked ice cubes. Pour 1 measure dark rum and 2 measures ginger beer over the ice and stir gently.

Cool Wind: put 4–6 cracked ice cubes into a mixing glass. Pour 3 measures vodka, 1 measure dry vermouth, 1 measure grapefruit juice, and ½ teaspoon triple sec over the ice. Stir well to mix, then strain into a chilled cocktail glass.

Fair and Warmer: put 4–6 cracked ice cubes into a glass. Dash clear Curaçao over the ice. Pour in 2 measures white rum and 1 measure sweet vermouth. Stir, then strain into a chilled cocktail glass.

Clear Skies Ahead: put 4–6 cracked ice cubes into a cocktail shaker. Pour 2 measures Scotch whisky, 1 measure lemon juice, ½ teaspoon sugar syrup (see page 11), and ½ teaspoon grenadine over the ice, and add 1 egg white. Shake vigorously until a frost forms, then strain into a chilled cocktail glass.

Damn the Weather: put 4–6 cracked ice cubes into a cocktail shaker. Pour 2 measures gin, ½ measure orange juice, 1 tablespoon sweet vermouth, and 2 teaspoons triple sec over the ice. Shake vigorously until a frost forms, then strain into a chilled cocktail glass.

Godfather

Amaretto is an Italian liqueur, so perhaps the inspiration for this cocktail comes from Don Corleone, the eponymous character in Mario Puzo's best-selling novel, unforgettably portrayed in the movie by Marlon Brando.

serves 1

4–6 cracked ice cubes

2 measures Scotch whisky

1 measure amaretto

❶ Fill a chilled highball glass with cracked ice cubes. Pour in the whisky and amaretto and stir to mix.

The family

Godmother: put 4–6 cracked ice cubes into a small, chilled glass. Pour 2 measures vodka and 1 measure amaretto over the ice. Stir to mix.

Godchild: put 4–6 crushed ice cubes into a blender and add 1½ measures amaretto, 1 measure vodka, and 1 measure light cream. Blend until smooth, then pour into a chilled champagne flute.

Goddaughter: put 4–6 crushed ice cubes into a blender and add 2 measures apple brandy, 1 measure amaretto, and 1 tablespoon apple sauce. Blend until smooth, then pour the mixture, without straining, into a chilled goblet. Sprinkle with ground cinnamon and serve with a straw.

Godson: put 4–6 cracked ice cubes into a chilled glass. Pour in 2 measures amaretto and top off with orange juice. Stir well to mix and decorate with a slice of orange.

Did you know?

Although flavored with almonds and herbal extracts, amaretto is actually made from apricot kernels.

Freedom Fighter

Crème Yvette is an American liqueur flavored with Parma violets. Because it has such a distinctive taste, you either love it or hate it—but it certainly makes pretty cocktails because it is such a lovely color. You could also use crème de violette, which is similar although not identical.

serves 1

4–6 cracked ice cubes
3 measures sloe gin
1 measure Crème Yvette
1 measure lemon juice
1 egg white

❶ Put the cracked ice cubes into a cocktail shaker. Pour the gin, Crème Yvette, and lemon juice over the ice, and add the egg white. Shake vigorously until a frost forms.
❷ Strain into a chilled wine glass.

Variations

Ping Pong: put 4–6 cracked ice cubes into a cocktail shaker. Pour 1 measure Crème Yvette, 1 measure sloe gin, and ½ measure lemon juice over the ice. Shake vigorously until a frost forms, then pour into a chilled cocktail glass.

Snowball: put 4–6 cracked ice cubes into a cocktail shaker. Pour 1½ measures gin, ½ measure Crème Yvette, ½ measure Anisette, ½ measure light cream, and ½ teaspoon sugar syrup (see page 11) over the ice. Shake vigorously until a frost forms, then pour into a chilled cocktail glass.

Union Jack: put 4–6 cracked ice cubes into a cocktail shaker. Pour in 3 measures dry gin and 1 measure Crème Yvette. Shake vigorously until a frost forms, then strain into a chilled cocktail glass. (For an alternative version of a Union Jack, see page 202.)

Jupiter: put 4–6 cracked ice cubes into a cocktail shaker. Pour 2 measures gin, 1 measure dry vermouth, ½ measure Crème Yvette, and ½ measure orange juice over the ice. Shake vigorously until a frost forms, then strain into a chilled wine glass.

Banshee

A surprising number of cocktails are named after ghouls, ghosts, and things that go bump in the night. It seems unlikely that this one will get you wailing (except with delight), but it might make your hair stand on end.

serves 1

4–6 cracked ice cubes
2 measures crème de banane
1 measure crème de cacao
1 measure light cream

❶ Put the cracked ice cubes into a cocktail shaker. Pour the crème de banane, crème de cacao, and light cream over the ice. Shake vigorously until a frost forms.
❷ Strain into a chilled wine glass.

Supernatural cocktails

Red Witch: put 4–6 cracked ice cubes into a cocktail shaker. Pour 2 measures Pernod and 1 measure blackcurrant cordial over the ice. Shake until a frost forms. Pour into a chilled wine glass and top off with chilled hard cider.

White Witch: put 4–6 cracked ice cubes into a cocktail shaker. Pour 2 measures white rum, 1 measure triple sec, and 1 measure white crème de cacao over the ice. Shake vigorously until a frost forms. Half fill a chilled glass with cracked ice cubes and strain the cocktail over them. Top off with sparkling mineral water.

Black Magic: put 4–6 cracked ice cubes into a cocktail shaker. Pour 2 measures vodka and 1 measure Tia Maria over the ice. Shake vigorously until a frost forms. Strain into a chilled cocktail glass.

Enchantment: put 4–6 cracked ice cubes into a cocktail shaker. Dash dry vermouth and orange bitters over the ice and pour in 2 measures Canadian whisky and 1 measure blue Curaçao. Shake vigorously until a frost forms, then strain into a chilled cocktail glass.

Leprechaun: put 4–6 crushed ice cubes into a blender. Pour in 2 measures Irish whiskey, 1 measure white rum, 1 measure lemon juice, ½ measure sloe gin, ½ teaspoon sugar syrup (see page 11), and ¼ peeled, pitted, and sliced peach. Blend until slushy. Pour into a small, chilled glass and decorate with raspberries.

Angel's Delight

This is a modern version of the classic pousse café, an unmixed, mixed drink, in that the ingredients form separate layers in the glass—provided you have a steady hand—to create a rainbow effect. You can drink it as a slammer (see page 170) or sip it in a more genteel manner.

serves 1

½ measure chilled grenadine
½ measure chilled triple sec
½ measure chilled sloe gin
½ measure chilled light cream

❶ Pour the grenadine into a chilled shot glass, pousse café glass, or champagne flute, then, with a steady hand, pour in the triple sec to make a second layer.
❷ Add the sloe gin to make a third layer and, finally, add the cream to float on top.

Variations

Angel's Kiss: pour ½ measure chilled crème de cacao into a chilled shot glass, pousse café glass, or champagne flute. With a steady hand, gently pour in ½ measure chilled sloe gin to make a second layer, then gently pour in ½ measure chilled brandy. Finally, gently pour in ½ measure chilled light cream.

Angel's Tit: pour ½ measure chilled white crème de cacao into a chilled shot glass, pousse café glass, or champagne flute. With a steady hand, pour in ½ measure chilled Maraschino to make a second layer and, finally, pour in ½ measure light cream to float on top. Decorate with a cocktail cherry.

Pousse Café: pour ½ measure chilled grenadine into chilled shot glass, pousse café glass, or champagne flute. With a steady hand, pour in ½ measure chilled white crème de cacao to make a second layer, followed by ½ measure chilled Maraschino to make a third layer. Pour in ½ measure chilled clear Curaçao, then pour in ½ measure chilled green crème de menthe to make a fifth layer. Finally, pour in ½ measure chilled brandy to float on top.

Pousse l'Amour: pour ½ measure chilled Maraschino into a chilled shot glass, pousse café glass, or champagne flute, then, with a steady hand, add 1 egg yolk to make a second layer. Then pour in ½ measure chilled Bénédictine to make a third layer and, finally, pour in ½ measure chilled brandy to float on top.

Pink Squirrel

Crème de noyaux has a wonderful, slightly bitter, nutty flavor, but is, in fact, made from peach and apricot kernels. It is usually served as a liqueur, but does combine well with some other ingredients in cocktails.

serves 1

4–6 cracked ice cubes
2 measures dark crème de cacao
1 measure crème de noyaux
1 measure light cream

❶ Put the cracked ice cubes into a cocktail shaker. Pour the crème de cacao, crème de noyaux, and light cream over the ice. Shake vigorously until a frost forms.
❷ Strain into a chilled cocktail glass.

In the pink

Pink Almond: put 4–6 cracked ice cubes into a cocktail shaker. Pour 2 measures blended American whiskey, 1 measure amaretto, ½ measure crème de noyaux, ½ measure cherry brandy, and 1 measure lemon juice over the ice. Shake vigorously until a frost forms. Strain into a chilled goblet and decorate with a slice of lemon.
Pink Pussycat: half fill a chilled glass with cracked ice cubes. Dash grenadine over the ice and pour in 2 measures gin. Top off with pineapple juice and decorate with a pineapple wedge.

Pink Heather: pour 1 measure Scotch whisky and 1 measure strawberry liqueur into a chilled champagne flute. Top off with chilled sparkling wine. Decorate with a strawberry.
Pink Whiskers: put 4–6 cracked ice cubes into a cocktail shaker. Dash grenadine over the ice and pour in 2 measures apricot brandy, 1 measure dry vermouth, and 2 measures orange juice. Shake vigorously until a frost forms, then strain the mixture into a chilled cocktail glass.

Full Monty

The expression "full monty," meaning not holding anything back, has been around for a long time, but was given a new lease of life by the highly successful British movie of the same title. However, you can keep your clothes on when mixing and drinking this cocktail.

serves 1

4–6 cracked ice cubes
1 measure vodka
1 measure Galliano
grated ginseng root, to decorate

❶ Put the cracked ice cubes into a cocktail shaker. Pour the vodka and Galliano over the ice. Shake vigorously until a frost forms.

❷ Strain into a chilled cocktail glass and sprinkle with grated ginseng root.

Cinematic cocktails

Back to the Future: put 4–6 cracked ice cubes into a cocktail shaker. Pour 2 measures gin, 1 measure slivovitz, and 1 measure lemon juice over the ice. Shake vigorously until a frost forms. Strain into a chilled cocktail glass.

Star Wars: put 4–6 cracked ice cubes into a cocktail shaker. Pour 2 measures gin, 2 measures lemon juice, 1 measure Galliano, and 1 measure crème de noyaux over the ice. Shake vigorously until a frost forms. Strain into a chilled cocktail glass.

Titanic: put 4–6 cracked ice cubes into a cocktail shaker. Pour 3 measures Mandarine Napoléon and 2 measures vodka over the ice. Shake vigorously until a frost forms. Half fill a chilled glass with cracked ice cubes and strain the cocktail over them. Top off with sparkling mineral water.

Last Mango in Paris: put 4–6 cracked ice cubes into a blender and add 2 measures vodka, 1 measure crème de framboise, 1 measure lime juice, ½ peeled, pitted, and chopped mango, and 2 halved strawberries. Blend until slushy. Pour into a chilled goblet and decorate with a slice of lime and a strawberry.

Star Bangled Spanner

Although only half measures of each spirit are used, there are seven layers of them, so this is quite a potent cocktail. It is probably fortunate that after getting your tongue around a couple, your hand will become too unsteady to pour more.

serves 1

½ measure chilled green Chartreuse
½ measure chilled triple sec
½ measure chilled cherry brandy
½ measure chilled crème violette
½ measure chilled yellow Chartreuse
½ measure chilled blue Curaçao
½ measure chilled brandy

❶ Pour the green Chartreuse into a chilled champagne flute, then, with a steady hand, gently pour in the triple sec to make a second layer.

❷ Gently add the cherry brandy to make a third layer, the crème violette to make a fourth, the yellow Chartreuse to make a fifth, and the Curaçao to make a sixth.

❸ Finally, float the brandy on top.

Fly the flag

Stars and Stripes: pour ¾ measure chilled cherry brandy into a chilled shot glass, pousse café glass, or champagne flute. With a steady hand, gently pour in 1½ measures chilled light cream to make a second layer and, finally, gently pour in ¾ measure chilled blue Curaçao.

Union Jack: pour 1 measure chilled Maraschino into a chilled shot glass. With a steady hand, gently pour in 1 measure

chilled blue Curaçao to make a second layer, and, finally, gently pour in 1 measure chilled grenadine. (For an alternative version of a Union Jack, see page 192.)

Tricolor: pour 1 measure chilled green crème de menthe into a chilled shot glass. With a steady hand, gently pour in 1 measure chilled Bailey's Irish Cream to make a second layer and, finally, gently pour in 1 measure chilled red Maraschino.

Did you know?

Chartreuse has been produced at the monastery of La Grande Chartreuse using the same recipe for 200 years. It contains more than 100 herbs and spices, but the exact formula remains a closely guarded secret.

Mad Dog

This cocktail is named in honor of Maximum Dog, who is himself a cocktail of breeds and who has been described as a cross between a goat and a monkey. However, he is not allowed to drink it.

serves 1

4–6 cracked ice cubes
1 measure white tequila
1 measure crème de banane
1 measure white crème de cacao
½ measure lime juice

To decorate
slice of lime
slice of banana
cocktail cherry

❶ Put the cracked ice cubes into a cocktail shaker. Pour the tequila, crème de banane, crème de cacao, and lime juice over the ice. Shake vigorously until a frost forms.

❷ Strain into a chilled cocktail glass and decorate with a lime slice, banana slice, and cocktail cherry.

Canine cocktails

Beagle: put 4–6 cracked ice cubes into a mixing glass. Dash kümmel and lemon juice over the ice and pour in 2 measures brandy and 1 measure cranberry juice. Stir well to mix, then strain into a chilled cocktail glass.

Great Dane: put 4–6 cracked ice cubes into a cocktail shaker. Pour 2 measures gin, 1 measure cherry brandy, ½ measure dry vermouth, and 1 teaspoon kirsch over the ice. Shake vigorously until a frost forms, then strain into a chilled cocktail glass. Decorate with a twist of lemon peel.

Bulldog: half fill a chilled glass with cracked ice cubes. Pour 1 measure gin and 2 measures orange juice over the ice and top off with chilled ginger ale. Stir gently to mix.

Bloodhound: put 4–6 crushed ice cubes into a blender and add 2 measures gin, 1 measure sweet vermouth, 1 measure dry vermouth, and 3 strawberries. Blend until smooth, then strain into a chilled cocktail glass.

Black Dog: put 4–6 cracked ice cubes into a mixing glass. Pour 3 measures bourbon, 1 measure dry vermouth, and ½ measure crème de cassis over the ice. Stir well to mix. Half fill a small, chilled glass with cracked ice cubes and strain the cocktail over them.

John Wood

Vermouth is an immensely useful flavoring for cocktails, because it contains more than fifty herbs and spices, ranging from cloves to rose petals, and combines well with many spirits, most notably gin. However, it has fallen in popularity as a base for cocktails over the last decade, but is now enjoying a revival of interest.

serves 1

4–6 cracked ice cubes
dash of Angostura bitters
2 measures sweet vermouth
½ measure kümmel
½ measure Irish whiskey
1 measure lemon juice

❶ Put the cracked ice cubes into a cocktail shaker. Dash Angostura bitters over the ice and pour in the vermouth, kümmel, whiskey, and lemon juice. Shake vigorously until a frost forms.
❷ Strain into a chilled wine glass.

Other vermouth cocktails

Bittersweet: put 4–6 cracked ice cubes into a cocktail shaker. Dash Angostura bitters and orange bitters over the ice and pour in 1½ measures sweet vermouth and 1½ measures dry vermouth. Shake vigorously until a frost forms. Fill a small, chilled glass with cracked ice and strain the cocktail over them. Decorate with a twist of orange peel.

Deep Sea: put 4–6 cracked ice cubes into a mixing glass. Dash Pernod and orange bitters over the ice. Pour in 1 measure dry vermouth and 1 measure gin. Shake until a frost forms, then strain into a chilled glass.

Did you know?

Many herb- and spice-flavored liqueurs, including kümmel, which is flavored with caraway seeds, are reputed to have digestive properties. This is a popularly held belief, particularly in France and Germany, but there is little, if any, scientific evidence to support it.

Which Way

Anise-flavored pastis, such as Pernod, are firm favorites in today's cocktail bars and often form the basis of almost lethally strong drinks.

serves 1

4–6 cracked ice cubes
1 measure Pernod
1 measure Anisette
1 measure brandy

❶ Put the cracked ice cubes into a cocktail shaker. Pour the Pernod, Anisette, and brandy over the ice. Shake vigorously until a frost forms.

❷ Strain into a chilled wine glass.

Variations

TNT: put 4–6 cracked ice cubes into a mixing glass. Pour 1 measure Pernod and 1 measure rye whiskey over the ice and stir well to mix. Strain into a chilled cocktail glass.

Victory: put 4–6 cracked ice cubes into a cocktail shaker. Pour 2 measures Pernod and 1 measure grenadine over the ice. Shake vigorously until a frost forms. Strain into a chilled glass and top off with sparkling mineral water.

Blanche: put 4–6 cracked ice cubes into a cocktail shaker. Pour 1 measure Pernod, 1 measure triple sec, and ½ measure clear Curaçao over the ice. Shake vigorously until a frost forms, then strain into a chilled cocktail glass.

Nineteen Pick-Me-Up: put 4–6 cracked ice cubes into a cocktail shaker. Dash Angostura bitters and orange bitters over the ice and pour in 2 measures Pernod, 1 measure gin, and ¼ teaspoon sugar syrup (see page 11). Shake vigorously until a frost forms. Half fill a glass with cracked ice cubes and strain the cocktail over them. Top off with sparkling mineral water.

Jade

You can tell good jade because it always feel cold to the touch—and that should apply to cocktails, too. No cocktail bar—whether in a hotel, pub, or at home—can ever have too much ice. Don't forget to chill the champagne for at least 2 hours before mixing.

serves 1

4–6 cracked ice cubes

dash of Angostura bitters

1/4 measure Midori

1/4 measure blue Curaçao

1/4 measure lime juice

chilled champagne, to top off

slice of lime, to decorate

❶ Put the cracked ice cubes into a cocktail shaker. Dash Angostura bitters over the ice and pour in the Midori, Curaçao, and lime juice. Shake vigorously until a frost forms.

❷ Strain into a chilled champagne flute. Top off with chilled champagne and decorate with a slice of lime.

Jewelry box

Diamond Head (to serve two): put 6–8 cracked ice cubes into a cocktail shaker. Pour 4 measures gin, 2 measures lemon juice, 1 measure apricot brandy, and 1 teaspoon sugar syrup (see page 11) over the ice, and add 1 egg white. Shake vigorously until a frost forms, then strain into two chilled cocktail glasses.

Diamond Fizz: put 4–6 cracked ice cubes into a cocktail shaker. Pour 2 measures gin, 1/2 measure lemon juice, and 1 teaspoon sugar syrup (see page 11) over the ice. Shake until a frost forms, then strain into a chilled champagne flute. Top off with chilled champagne.

Sapphire Martini: put 4–6 cracked ice cubes into a mixing glass. Pour 2 measures gin and 1/2 measure blue Curaçao over the ice. Stir well to mix, then strain into a chilled cocktail glass. Decorate with a blue cocktail cherry. (For a Martini and other variations, see page 40.)

Topaz Martini: put 4–6 cracked ice cubes into a mixing glass. Pour 2 measures gin and 1/2 measure orange Curaçao over the ice. Stir to mix. Strain into a chilled cocktail glass. Decorate with a slice of lemon.

Emerald Isle: put 4–6 cracked ice cubes into a mixing glass. Dash Angostura bitters over the ice and pour in 2 1/2 measures gin and 2 teaspoons green crème de menthe. Stir well to mix, then strain into a chilled cocktail glass. Decorate with a green cocktail olive.

Caribbean Champagne

Both rum and bananas are naturally associated with the tropics, but wine does not spring so readily to mind when the Caribbean is mentioned. However, remember that France and many Caribbean islands, such as Martinique and Guadeloupe, share a long history.

serves 1

½ measure white rum
½ measure crème de banane
chilled champagne, to top off
slice of banana, to decorate

❶ Pour the rum and crème de banane into a chilled champagne flute. Top off with champagne.
❷ Stir gently to mix and decorate with a slice of banana.

"Champagne for my sham friends"

American Flyer: put 4–6 cracked ice cubes into a cocktail shaker. Pour in 1½ measures white rum, 1 tablespoon lime juice, and ½ teaspoon sugar syrup (see page 11). Shake vigorously until a frost forms. Strain the mixture into a chilled champagne flute and top off with chilled champagne or sparkling white wine.

Chicago: rub the rim of a large, chilled brandy glass with a wedge of lemon and then dip in superfine sugar to frost. Put 4–6 cracked ice cubes into a mixing glass. Dash triple sec and Angostura bitters over the ice and pour in 2 measures brandy. Stir and strain into the prepared glass. Top off with chilled champagne or sparkling white wine.

Dawn: pour 1 measure chilled champagne or sparkling white wine, 1 measure chilled dry sherry, and 1 measure chilled lime juice into a chilled cocktail glass. Stir to mix.

Millennium Cocktail

A good way to start the twenty-first century—and an even better way to carry on—is to drink this sparkling cocktail at regular intervals.

serves 1

4-6 cracked ice cubes
1 measure raspberry vodka
1 measure fresh raspberry juice
1 measure orange juice
chilled champagne, to top off
raspberries, to decorate

❶ Put the cracked ice cubes into a cocktail shaker. Pour the vodka, raspberry juice, and orange juice over the ice. Shake vigorously until a frost forms.

❷ Strain into a chilled champagne flute and top off with chilled champagne. Stir gently to mix and decorate with raspberries.

Time and tide

Leap Year: put 4-6 cracked ice cubes into a cocktail shaker. Pour 2 measures gin, ½ measure Grand Marnier, ½ measure sweet vermouth, and ½ teaspoon lemon juice over the ice. Shake until a frost forms, then strain into a chilled cocktail glass.

Thanksgiving Special: put 4-6 cracked ice cubes into a cocktail shaker. Pour 2 measures gin, 1½ measures apricot brandy, 1 measure dry vermouth, and ½ measure lemon juice over the ice.

Shake vigorously until a frost forms, then strain into a chilled cocktail glass. Decorate with a cocktail cherry.

Cool Yule Martini: put 4-6 cracked ice cubes into a cocktail shaker. Pour 3 measures vodka, ½ measure dry vermouth, and 1 teaspoon peppermint schnapps over the ice. Shake until a frost forms, then strain into a chilled cocktail glass. Decorate with a peppermint candy cane. (For a Martini and other variations, see page 40.)

Did you know?

Only wine from the Champagne region of France and produced by the Champagne method may be called Champagne. It is very expensive, and, to some, it is sacrilege to mix it with other ingredients, so good-quality, less expensive sparkling wines can be substituted, but make sure they are dry.

Nonalcoholic Cocktails

Lip Smacker

So many delicious ingredients are available today, that nonalcoholic cocktails really have come into their own. This one has all the kick of an alcoholic cocktail.

serves 1

4–6 crushed ice cubes

1 small tomato, peeled, seeded, and chopped

1 measure orange juice

2 tsp lime juice

1 scallion, chopped

1 small, fresh, red chile, seeded and chopped

pinch of superfine sugar

pinch of salt

dash of Tabasco sauce

To decorate

slice of lime and a chile rosette (see below)

❶ Put the crushed ice, tomato, orange juice, lime juice, scallion, and chile in a blender and process until smooth.

❷ Pour into a chilled glass, season to taste with sugar, salt, and Tabasco sauce and stir to mix. Decorate with a slice of lime and a chile rosette. To make a rosette, use a sharp knife to make 5 or 6 cuts ½ inch/1 cm from the stalk end to the tip of a long, thin chile. Place in iced water for 30 minutes, until fanned out.

Variation

Open Prairie Oyster: dash Tabasco sauce and white wine vinegar into a glass. Pour in 1 teaspoon Worcestershire sauce and 1 measure tomato juice. Stir and add 1 egg yolk. Drink down in one. (For a Prairie Oyster, see page 22.)

Did you know?

Sun-ripened tomatoes have a much sweeter and more concentrated flavor than those grown under glass or in polytunnels.

Bloody January

Generally, the best nonalcoholic cocktails are originals rather than pale and often insipid copies of their traditional, alcoholic cousins. This nonalcoholic version of the Bloody Mary is one of the exceptions and has some of the kick of the classic cocktail.

serves 1

4–6 crushed ice cubes

1 medium bell pepper, seeded, and coarsely chopped

2 large tomatoes, peeled, seeded, and coarsely chopped

1 fresh green chili, seeded

juice of 1 lime

salt and freshly ground black pepper

celery stalk, to decorate

❶ Put the crushed ice cubes into a blender and add the bell pepper, tomatoes, chili, and lime juice. Blend until smooth.

❷ Pour into a chilled highball glass and season to taste with salt and pepper. Decorate with a celery stalk.

Variations

Virgin Mary: put 4–6 cracked ice cubes into a cocktail shaker. Dash Worcestershire sauce and Tabasco sauce over the ice, pour in 4 measures tomato juice and 1 measure lime juice, and add ¼ teaspoon horseradish sauce. Shake vigorously until a frost forms. Strain into a chilled glass and season to taste with salt and freshly ground black pepper. Decorate with a wedge of lime.

Ferdinand the Bull: put 4–6 cracked ice cubes into a cocktail shaker. Dash Worcestershire sauce and Tabasco sauce over the ice and pour in 4 measures tomato juice, 4 measures chilled bouillon, and 1 measure lime juice. Shake until a frost forms. Half fill a chilled glass with cracked ice cubes and strain the cocktail over them. Season to taste with salt and freshly ground black pepper and decorate with a slice of lime.

Texas Virgin: put 4–6 cracked ice cubes into a cocktail shaker. Dash Worcestershire sauce and Tabasco sauce over the ice and pour in 1 measure lime juice and 1 measure barbecue sauce. Shake vigorously until a frost forms, then pour into a chilled glass. Top off with tomato sauce and stir. Decorate with a slice of lime and a pickled jalapeño chili. (For a Bloody Mary and other alcoholic variations, see page 86.)

Carrot Cream

Although carrots are vegetables, they have a strong hint of sweetness that makes them or their juice an excellent and delicious basis for mixed drinks. Since raw carrots are packed with vitamins and minerals, they are a healthy option, too.

serves 1

4–6 cracked ice cubes

2 measures carrot juice

2½ measures light cream

1 measure orange juice

1 egg yolk

slice of orange, to decorate

❶ Put the cracked ice cubes into a cocktail shaker. Pour the carrot juice, cream, and orange juice over the ice and add the egg yolk. Shake vigorously until a frost forms.

❷ Strain into a chilled glass and decorate with the orange slice.

Variations

Carrot Cocktail: put 6–8 crushed ice cubes into a blender and add 3 measures pineapple juice, 2 coarsely chopped small carrots, and ¼ cup crushed pineapple. Blend until slushy. Pour the mixture, without straining, into a chilled glass.

Delirious Donkey: put 6–8 crushed ice cubes into a blender and add 3 measures orange juice, 1 coarsely chopped large carrot, and a 2 inch/5 cm piece of peeled and coarsely chopped cucumber. Blend until slushy. Pour, without straining, into a chilled glass and decorate with a slice of cucumber and a slice of orange.

Clam Digger

This is another good cocktail for a Sunday brunch, when alcoholic drinks can be too soporific and you end up wasting the rest of the day, but you still want something to wake up the taste buds and set them tingling.

serves 1

10–12 cracked ice cubes

Tabasco sauce

Worcestershire sauce

4 measures tomato juice

4 measures clam juice

¼ tsp horseradish sauce

celery salt and freshly ground black pepper

To decorate

celery stalk

wedge of lime

❶ Put 4–6 cracked ice cubes into a cocktail shaker. Dash the Tabasco sauce and Worcestershire sauce over the ice, pour in the tomato juice and clam juice, and add the horseradish sauce. Shake vigorously until a frost forms.

❷ Fill a chilled Collins glass with cracked ice cubes and strain the cocktail over them. Season to taste with celery salt and pepper and decorate with a celery stalk and lime wedge.

Variations

New England Party: put 6–8 crushed ice cubes into a blender and dash Tabasco sauce, Worcestershire sauce, and lemon juice over the ice. Add 1 medium chopped carrot, 2 chopped celery stalks, 1¼ cups tomato juice, and ⅔ cup clam juice. Blend until smooth. Transfer to a pitcher, cover with plastic wrap, and chill in the refrigerator for about 1 hour. Pour the cocktail into 2 chilled glasses and season with salt and freshly ground black pepper to taste. Decorate with cocktail olives speared on a cocktail stick.

Bartender's Tip

A commercial product called Clamato Juice—a mix of tomato and clam juices—is available from some supermarkets and delicatessens and can be substituted for the separate ingredients.

Faux Kir

A nonalcoholic version of a classic wine cocktail, this drink is just as colorful and tasty. French and Italian fruit syrups are often the best quality and have the most flavor.

serves 1

1 measure chilled raspberry syrup
chilled white grape juice, to top off
twist of lemon peel, to decorate

❶ Pour the raspberry syrup into a chilled wine glass. Top off with the grape juice.
❷ Stir well to mix and decorate with the lemon twist.

Variations

Faux Kir Royale: put 4–6 cracked ice cubes into a mixing glass. Pour 1½ measures raspberry syrup over the ice. Stir well to mix, then strain into a wine glass. Top off with chilled sparkling apple juice and stir.

Knicks Victory Cooler: half fill a tall, chilled glass with cracked ice cubes. Pour 2 measures apricot juice over the ice, top off with raspberry soda, and stir gently. Decorate with a spiral of orange peel and fresh raspberries.

Cocoberry: rub ½ cup raspberries through a metal strainer with the back of a spoon and transfer the purée to a blender. Add 4–6 crushed ice cubes, 1 measure coconut cream, and ⅔ cup pineapple juice. Blend

until smooth, then pour the mixture, without straining, into a chilled glass. Decorate with pineapple wedges and fresh raspberries.

All Shook Up: put ½ cup mixed strawberries and raspberries, 4 measures chilled milk, 4 measures chilled plain yogurt, and 1 teaspoon rosewater into a blender. Blend until smooth and then pour the mixture into a chilled glass. Stir in ½ teaspoon clear honey and decorate with a strawberry and a raspberry. Serve with straws.

Bartender's Tip
For a Kir and other alcoholic variations, see page 106.

Eye of the Hurricane

In recent years, a vast range of fruit juices and syrups has become widely available. These can extend the range of the cocktail bar and are particularly useful for nonalcoholic mixed drinks, which were once heavily dependent on the somewhat tired old favorites of orange, lemon, and lime juices.

serves 1

4–6 cracked ice cubes

2 measures passion fruit syrup

1 measure lime juice

bitter lemon, to top off

slice of lemon, to decorate

❶ Put the cracked ice cubes into a mixing glass. Pour the syrup and lime juice over the ice and stir well to mix.

❷ Strain into a chilled glass and top off with bitter lemon. Stir gently and decorate with the lemon slice.

Variations

Tropical Storm: put 4–6 cracked ice cubes into a cocktail shaker. Pour 2 measures pineapple juice, 2 measures lime juice, 1 measure passion fruit syrup, and ½ teaspoon orgeat over the ice. Shake vigorously until a frost forms. Strain into a small, chilled glass and decorate with a pineapple wedge.

Daydream: half fill a tall, chilled glass with cracked ice cubes. Pour 1½ measures passion fruit syrup over the ice and top off with chilled orange juice. Stir gently to mix and sprinkle with freshly grated nutmeg.

Quiet Passion: put 4–6 cracked ice cubes into a cocktail shaker. Pour 4 measures grapefruit juice, 4 measures white grape juice, and 1 measure passion fruit juice over the ice. Shake vigorously until a frost forms. Half fill a chilled glass with cracked ice cubes and strain the cocktail over them. Decorate with a slice of lime.

Juicy Julep

Taken from the Arabic word, meaning a rose syrup, it seems likely that this was always intended to be a nonalcoholic drink and that it was bourbon-drinkers who hijacked the term, not the other way around. (For a Mint Julep and other alcoholic variations, see page 30.)

serves 1

4–6 cracked ice cubes
1 measure orange juice
1 measure pineapple juice
1 measure lime juice
½ measure raspberry syrup
4 crushed fresh mint leaves
ginger ale, to top off
sprig of fresh mint, to decorate

❶ Put the cracked ice cubes into a cocktail shaker. Pour the orange juice, pineapple juice, lime juice, and raspberry syrup over the ice and add the mint leaves. Shake vigorously until a frost forms.
❷ Strain into a chilled Collins glass, top off with ginger ale, and stir gently. Decorate with a fresh mint sprig.

Other junior relatives

Salty Puppy: mix equal quantities of granulated sugar and coarse salt on a saucer. Rub the rim of a small, chilled glass with a wedge of lime, then dip in the sugar/salt mixture to frost. Fill the glass with cracked ice cubes and pour ½ measure lime juice over them. Top off with grapefruit juice. (For a Salty Dog and other alcoholic variations, see page 94.)

Baby Bellini: pour 2 measures peach juice and 1 measure lemon juice into a chilled champagne flute and stir well. Top off with sparkling apple juice and stir. (For a Bellini and Bellinitini, see page 106.)

Cool Collins: put 6 fresh mint leaves into a tall, chilled glass and add 1 teaspoon superfine sugar and 2 measures lemon juice. Crush the leaves with a spoon until the sugar has dissolved. Fill the glass with cracked ice cubes and top off with sparkling water. Stir gently and decorate with a fresh mint sprig and a slice of lemon. (For a Tom Collins and other alcoholic variations, see page 48.)

Sunrise: put 4–6 cracked ice cubes into a chilled glass. Pour 2 measures orange juice, 1 measure lemon juice, and 1 measure grenadine over the ice. Stir well to mix and then top off with sparkling mineral water. (For a Tequila Sunrise and other alcoholic variations, see page 82.)

Island Cooler

Nothing could be more refreshing on a hot summer's day than this colorful combination of tropical fruit juices. To get into a party mood, go to town with the decoration with a cocktail parasol, swizzle stick, and straws, as well as fresh fruit, if you like.

serves 1

8–10 cracked ice cubes
2 measures orange juice
1 measure lemon juice
1 measure pineapple juice
1 measure papaya juice
½ tsp grenadine
sparkling mineral water, to top off

To decorate
pineapple wedges
cocktail cherries

❶ Put 4–6 cracked ice cubes into a cocktail shaker. Pour the orange juice, lemon juice, pineapple juice, papaya juice, and grenadine over the ice. Shake vigorously until a frost forms.

❷ Half fill a chilled Collins glass with cracked ice cubes and pour the cocktail over them. Top off with sparkling mineral water and stir gently. Decorate with pineapple wedges and cocktail cherries speared on a cocktail stick.

Another exotic destination

Caribbean Cocktail: put 4–6 crushed ice cubes into a blender and add a dash of lime juice, 4 measures orange juice, the coarsely chopped flesh of ½ mango, and ½ peeled and sliced banana. Blend until smooth. Half fill a chilled glass with cracked ice cubes and pour the cocktail over them. Decorate with a slice of lime.

Did you know?

Papaya seeds, although edible, have a very peppery flavor so, if you are squeezing the juice yourself, it is important to remove all of them. Papaya juice is commercially available.

Little Prince

Sparkling apple juice is a particularly useful ingredient in nonalcoholic cocktails because it adds flavor and color, as well as fizz. Try using it as a substitute for champagne in nonalcoholic versions of such cocktails as Buck's Fizz (see page 112).

serves 1

4–6 cracked ice cubes
1 measure apricot juice
1 measure lemon juice
2 measures sparkling apple juice
twist of lemon peel, to decorate

❶ Put the cracked ice cubes into a mixing glass. Pour the apricot juice, lemon juice, and apple juice over the ice and stir well.
❷ Strain into a chilled highball glass and decorate with the lemon twist.

An apple a day

Apple Frazzle: put 4–6 cracked ice cubes into a cocktail shaker. Pour 4 measures apple juice, 1 teaspoon sugar syrup (see page 11), and ½ teaspoon lemon juice over the ice. Shake vigorously until a frost forms. Strain into a chilled glass and top off with sparkling mineral water.

Bite of the Apple: put 4–6 crushed ice cubes into a blender and add 5 measures apple juice, 1 measure lime juice, ½ teaspoon orgeat, and 1 tablespoon apple sauce or apple purée. Blend until smooth, then pour into a chilled glass. Sprinkle with ground cinnamon.

Prohibition Punch (to serve 25): pour 3¾ cups apple juice, 1½ cups lemon juice, and ½ cup sugar syrup (see page 11) into a large pitcher. Add cracked ice cubes and 9 cups ginger ale. Stir gently to mix. Serve in chilled glasses, decorated with slices of orange and with straws.

Red Apple Sunset: put 4–6 cracked ice cubes into a cocktail shaker. Dash grenadine over the ice and pour in 2 measures apple juice and 2 measures grapefruit juice. Shake vigorously until a frost forms. Strain into a chilled cocktail glass.

Sparkling Peach Melba

Peach Melba was a dessert invented by Escoffier, chef at the Savoy Hotel in London, in honor of the Australian opera singer Dame Nellie Melba. This simple, but perfect partnership of peaches and raspberries has become a classic combination, now transformed into a wonderfully refreshing cocktail.

serves 1

¼ cup frozen raspberries
4 measures peach juice
sparkling mineral water, to top off

❶ Rub the raspberries through a wire strainer with the back of a wooden spoon. Transfer the purée to a cocktail shaker.

❷ Pour the peach juice into the cocktail shaker and shake vigorously until a frost forms.

❸ Strain into a tall, chilled glass and top off with sparkling mineral water. Stir gently.

Life's a peach

Peachy Melba: put 4–6 cracked ice cubes into a cocktail shaker. Pour 3 measures peach juice, 1 measure lemon juice, 1 measure lime juice, and 1 measure grenadine over the ice. Shake until a frost forms. Strain into a small, chilled glass and decorate with a slice of peach.

Under the Boardwalk: put 4–6 crushed ice cubes into a blender. Add 2 measures lemon juice, ½ teaspoon sugar syrup (see page 11), and ½ peeled and chopped peach. Blend until slushy, then pour into a chilled glass. Top off with sparkling mineral water and stir gently. Decorate with raspberries.

Peachy Cream: put 4–6 cracked ice cubes into a cocktail shaker. Pour 2 measures peach juice and 2 measures light cream into a cocktail shaker. Shake vigorously until a frost forms. Half fill a small, chilled glass with cracked ice cubes and then strain the cocktail over them.

Bartender's Tip

Using frozen raspberries ensures a convenient supply at any time of year. If you prefer to use fresh raspberries, put 4–6 crushed ice cubes into the cocktail shaker before adding the purée.

California Smoothie

Smoothies of all sorts—alcoholic and nonalcoholic—have become immensely popular in the last two or three years. The secret of success is to blend them on medium speed until just smooth.

serves 1

1 banana, peeled and thinly sliced

½ cup strawberries

½ cup pitted dates

4½ tsp honey

1 cup orange juice

4–6 crushed ice cubes

❶ Put the banana, strawberries, dates, and honey into a blender and blend until smooth.

❷ Add the orange juice and crushed ice cubes and blend again until smooth. Pour into a chilled Collins glass.

Smooth as silk

Apricot Smoothie: put 4–6 crushed ice cubes into a blender. Add 2 peeled, pitted, and chopped apricots, 2 measures pineapple juice, 1 measure lime juice, and 1 measure cherry syrup. Blend until smooth, then pour into a chilled glass.

Mango Smoothie: put 4–6 crushed ice cubes into a blender and add 1 measure lime juice, 1 small, peeled, pitted, and chopped mango, and 2 hulled strawberries. Blend until smooth, then pour into a chilled goblet. Decorate with a strawberry and a slice of lime.

Papaya Smoothie: put 4–6 crushed ice cubes into a blender and add ¾ cup orange juice, 1 peeled and sliced banana, ½ peeled and diced papaya, 1½ teaspoons clear honey, and ¼ teaspoon vanilla extract. Blend until smooth, then pour into a chilled glass.

Pineapple Smoothie: put 4–6 crushed ice cubes into a blender and add 2 measures pineapple juice, 1 measure lime juice, and ½ banana. Blend until smooth, then pour the mixture into a chilled glass.

Italian Soda

Available from Italian delicatessens and some supermarkets, Italian syrup comes in a wide variety of flavors, including a range of fruit and nuts. French syrups are similar and also include many different flavors. You can substitute your favorite for the hazelnut used here and vary the quantity depending on how sweet you like your drinks.

serves 1

6–8 cracked ice cubes
1–1½ measures hazelnut syrup
sparkling mineral water, to top off
slice of lime, to decorate

❶ Fill a chilled Collins glass with cracked ice cubes. Pour the hazelnut syrup over the ice and top off with sparkling mineral water.
❷ Stir gently and decorate with the lime slice.

Variations

Heavenly Days: put 4–6 cracked ice cubes into a cocktail shaker. Pour 2 measures hazelnut syrup, 2 measures lemon juice, and 1 teaspoon grenadine over the ice. Shake vigorously until a frost forms. Half fill a glass with cracked ice cubes and strain the cocktail over them. Top off with sparkling mineral water. Stir gently and then decorate with a slice of orange.

Cherry Stone: put 4–6 cracked ice cubes into a cocktail shaker. Pour 2 measures cherry syrup and 2 measures lime juice over the ice. Shake vigorously until a frost forms. Half fill a glass with cracked ice cubes and strain the cocktail over them. Top off with sparkling apple juice. Stir gently and decorate with cocktail cherries.

Orgeat Cola: put 4–6 cracked ice cubes into a cocktail shaker. Pour 2 measures orgeat and 2 measures lime juice over the ice. Shake vigorously until a frost forms. Half fill a glass with cracked ice cubes and strain the cocktail over them. Top off with cola. Stir gently and decorate with a pineapple wedge.

Grapefruit Cooler

This is a wonderfully refreshing drink that is ideal for serving at a family barbecue. Start making this at least two hours before you want to serve it to have plenty of time for the mint to steep in the syrup.

serves 6

2 oz/60 g fresh mint
2 measures sugar syrup (see page 11)
2 cups grapefruit juice
4 measures lemon juice
about 30 cracked ice cubes
sparkling mineral water, to top off
sprigs of fresh mint, to decorate

❶ Crush the fresh mint leaves and place in a small bowl. Add the sugar syrup and stir well. Set aside for at least 2 hours to soak, mashing the mint with a spoon from time to time.

❷ Strain the syrup into a pitcher and add the grapefruit juice and lemon juice. Cover with plastic wrap and chill in the refrigerator for at least 2 hours.

❸ To serve, fill six chilled Collins glasses with cracked ice. Divide the cocktail among the glasses and top off with sparkling mineral water. Decorate with fresh mint sprigs.

Cool it

Coconut Cooler: put 4–6 cracked ice cubes into a cocktail shaker. Pour 2 measures coconut milk and 2 measures lime juice over the ice and shake until a frost forms. Half fill a chilled glass with cracked ice cubes and then strain the cocktail over them. Decorate with a sprig of fresh mint.

Did you know?

There is a green-skinned grapefruit variety called "Sweetie" that is less sharp than the yellow-skinned fruits. Pink grapefruit is also slightly milder in flavor.

Cranberry Punch

A sophisticated, nonalcoholic punch, this can also be served hot for a winter party—it is especially good for celebrating the New Year—as well as chilled in the summer.

serves 10

2½ cups cranberry juice

2½ cups orange juice

⅔ cup water

½ tsp ground ginger

¼ tsp ground cinnamon

¼ tsp freshly grated nutmeg

cracked ice cubes or block of ice, optional

To decorate (cold punch):

fresh cranberries

1 egg white, lightly beaten

superfine sugar

sprigs of fresh mint

To decorate (hot punch):

slices of lemon

slices of orange

Fresh and fruity

Cape Cod Sunrise (serves 1): put 4–6 cracked ice cubes into a cocktail shaker. Pour 3 measures cranberry juice and 1 measure lime juice over the ice and shake vigorously until a frost forms. Pour into a chilled wine glass and decorate with a slice of lime.

❶ First prepare the decoration, if you are planning to serve the punch cold. Dip the cranberries, one by one, in the egg white and let the excess drip off, then roll them in the sugar to frost, shaking off any excess. Set aside on baking parchment to dry. Brush the mint leaves with egg white and then dip in the sugar to frost, shaking off any excess. Set aside on baking parchment to dry.

❷ Put the cranberry juice, orange juice, water, ginger, cinnamon, and nutmeg in a pan and bring to a boil. Lower the heat and simmer for 5 minutes.

❸ Remove the pan from the heat. If serving hot, ladle into warmed individual punch glasses or pour into a warmed punch bowl. Decorate with slices of lemon and orange.

❹ If serving the punch cold, set aside to cool, then pour into a pitcher, cover with plastic wrap, and chill in the refrigerator for at least 2 hours, until required.

❺ To serve the cold punch, place cracked ice or a block of ice in a chilled punch bowl and pour in the punch. Alternatively, fill glasses with cracked ice and then pour the punch over them. Decorate with the frosted cranberries and mint leaves.

Mocha Slush

Definitely for people with a sweet tooth, this is a chocoholic's dream and is popular with adults, as well as children.

serves 1

4–6 crushed ice cubes
2 measures coffee syrup
1 measure chocolate syrup
4 measures milk
grated chocolate, to decorate

❶ Put the crushed ice cubes into a blender and add the coffee syrup, chocolate syrup, and milk. Blend until slushy.

❷ Pour into a chilled goblet and sprinkle with grated chocolate.

Sweet dreams

Chocomint Slush: put 4–6 crushed ice cubes into a blender and add 2 measures chocolate syrup, 1 measure peppermint syrup, and 4 measures milk. Blend until slushy. Pour the mixture into a chilled goblet. Decorate with a sprig of fresh mint.

Chocolate Champers: pour 1½ measures chocolate syrup into a tall, chilled glass. Add 3½ measures chilled milk and stir well to mix. Top off with club soda and stir vigorously.

Alexander's Daughter: put 4–6 cracked ice cubes into a cocktail shaker. Pour 1 measure chocolate syrup, 1 measure ginger syrup, and 1 measure light cream over the ice. Shake vigorously until a frost forms, then strain the mixture into a chilled cocktail glass. Sprinkle with freshly ground nutmeg. (For an Alexander and other alcoholic variations, see page 46).

Black Forest: pour 1 measure chocolate syrup into a small, chilled glass, such as a sherry or liqueur glass. Pour 1 measure cherry syrup on top and then pour in 1 measure heavy cream.

Shirley Temple

This is one of the most famous of classic nonalcoholic cocktails. Shirley Temple Black became a respected diplomat, but this cocktail dates from the days when she was an immensely popular child movie star in the 1930s.

serves 1

8–10 cracked ice cubes
2 measures lemon juice
½ measure grenadine
½ measure sugar syrup (see page 11)
ginger ale, to top off

To decorate
slice of orange
cocktail cherry

❶ Put 4–6 cracked ice cubes into a cocktail shaker. Pour the lemon juice, grenadine, and sugar syrup over the ice and shake vigorously.

❷ Half fill a small, chilled glass with cracked ice cubes and strain the cocktail over them. Top off with ginger ale. Decorate with an orange slice and a cocktail cherry.

Other classics

St. Clements: put 6–8 cracked ice cubes into a chilled glass. Pour 2 measures orange juice and 2 measures bitter lemon over the ice. Stir gently and decorate with a slice of orange and a slice of lemon.

Black and Tan: pour ⅔ cup chilled ginger ale into a chilled glass. Add ⅔ cup chilled ginger beer. Do not stir. Decorate with a wedge of lime.

Tea Punch: put 4–6 cracked ice cubes into a mixing glass. Pour 3 measures cold black tea, 3 measures orange juice, 3 measures sparkling apple juice, and 1½ measures lemon juice over the ice. Stir well to mix, then pour into a tall, chilled glass. Decorate with a slice of lemon.

Beachcomber: put 4–6 cracked ice cubes into a cocktail shaker. Pour ⅔ cup guava juice, 2 measures lime juice, and 1 measure raspberry syrup over the ice. Shake vigorously until a frost forms, then pour into a chilled glass.

Soft Sangria

This is a version of the well-known Spanish wine cup that has caught out many an unwary tourist because it seems so innocuous, whereas it is actually very potent. A Soft Sangria poses no such danger of unexpected inebriation, but is just as refreshing and flavorsome. Make sure all the ingredients are thoroughly chilled before mixing them.

serves 20

6 cups red grape juice

1¼ cups orange juice

3 measures cranberry juice

2 measures lemon juice

2 measures lime juice

4 measures sugar syrup (see page 11)

block of ice

To decorate

slices of lemon

slices of orange

slices of lime

❶ Put the grape juice, orange juice, cranberry juice, lemon juice, lime juice, and sugar syrup into a chilled punch bowl and stir well.

❷ Add the ice and decorate with the slices of lemon, orange, and lime.

Down Mexico way

Sangrita Seca (to serve 6): pour 2 cups tomato juice, 1 cup orange juice, 3 measures lime juice, ½ measure Tabasco sauce, and 2 teaspoons Worcestershire sauce into a pitcher. Add 1 seeded and finely chopped jalapeño chile. Season to taste with celery salt and freshly ground white pepper and stir well to mix. Cover with plastic wrap and chill in the refrigerator for at least 1 hour. To serve, half fill chilled glasses with cracked ice cubes and strain the cocktail over them.

Did you know?

The easiest way to make a large block of ice is to freeze an ordinary ice cube tray filled with water, having first removed the compartments.

Melon Medley

Choose a very ripe, sweet-fleshed melon, such as a cantaloupe, for this lovely, fresh-tasting cocktail. This melon drink is perfect for sipping on a hot evening.

serves 1

4–6 crushed ice cubes
½ cup diced melon flesh
4 measures orange juice
½ measure lemon juice

❶ Put the crushed ice cubes into a blender and add the diced melon. Pour in the orange juice and lemon juice. Blend until slushy.

❷ Pour into a chilled Collins glass.

Sweet and juicy

River Cruise (to serve 6): put 8 cups diced cantaloupe melon flesh into a blender or food processor and process to a smooth purée. Scrape the purée into a pitcher. Put the peel and juice of 2 lemons and 2 tablespoons sugar into a small pan. Heat gently, stirring until the sugar has dissolved. Pour the lemon syrup over the melon purée and set aside to cool, then cover with plastic wrap, and chill in the refrigerator for at least 2 hours. To serve, half fill six chilled glasses with cracked ice. Stir the melon mixture and divide it among the glasses. Top off with sparkling mineral water and decorate with melon wedges and cocktail cherries.

Kool Kevin: put 4–6 crushed ice cubes into a blender and add ½ cup diced cantaloupe melon flesh, 1 measure grenadine, and 1 measure heavy cream. Blend until smooth then pour into a small, chilled glass. Add 1 measure ginger ale and stir gently. Sprinkle with ground ginger and decorate with a wedge of melon.

Glossary

Amaretto: almond-flavored liqueur from Italy

Amer Picon: French apéritif bitters, flavored with orange and gentian

Angostura bitters: rum-based bitters from Trinidad

Anisette: French liqueur, flavored with anise, cilantro, and other herbs

Applejack: North American name for apple brandy (see Fruit brandy)

Aquavit: Scandinavian grain spirit, usually flavored with caraway

Armagnac: French brandy produced in Gascony—rarely used for cocktails

Bacardi: leading brand of white rum, originally from Cuba and now produced in Bermuda—also the name of a cocktail

Bailey's Irish Cream: Irish, whiskey-based, chocolate-flavored liqueur

Bénédictine: French, monastic liqueur flavored with herbs, spices, and honey

Bitters: a flavor-enhancer made from berries, roots, and herbs

Bourbon: American whiskey made from a mash that must contain at least 51 percent corn

Brandy: spirit distilled from fermented grapes, although many fruit brandies are based on other fruits (see Fruit brandy)

Calvados: French apple brandy from Normandy

Campari: Italian bitters flavored with quinine

Champagne: French sparkling wine from La Champagne, produced under strictly controlled conditions

Chartreuse: French monastic liqueur flavored with a secret recipe of herbs—green Chartreuse is stronger than yellow

Cobbler: long, mixed drink traditionally based on sherry but now made from spirits and other ingredients

Coconut liqueur: coconut-flavored, spirit-based liqueur—Malibu is the best-known brand

Coffee liqueur: coffee-flavored, spirit-based liqueur—Tia Maria, based on Jamaican rum, and Kahlúa from Mexico are the best-known brands

Cointreau: best-selling brand of triple sec (see Triple sec), flavored with sweet Mediterranean oranges and Caribbean bitter orange peel

Collins: a spirit-based cocktail topped off with a carbonated soda, such as ginger ale

Crème de banane: banana-flavored liqueur

Crème de cacao: French, chocolate-flavored liqueur, produced in various strengths and colors

Crème de cassis: blackcurrant-flavored liqueur, mainly from France

Crème de framboise: raspberry-flavored liqueur

Crème de menthe: mint-flavored liqueur—may be white or green

Crème de noyaux: liqueur made from apricot and peach kernels

Crème violette: violet-flavored liqueur

Crème Yvette: American Parma violet-flavored liqueur

Curaçao: orange-flavored liqueur, produced mainly in France and The Netherlands, but originating from the Caribbean—available in a range of colors including white, orange, and blue

Drambuie: Scotch whisky-based liqueur, flavored with honey and heather

Dry gin: see Gin

Dubonnet: wine-based apéritif, flavored with quinine—available red and blonde

Eau-de-vie: spirit distilled from fruit—tends to be used (wrongly) as interchangeable with fruit brandy

Falernum: Caribbean syrup flavored with fruit and spices

Fernet Branca: Italian liqueur with a bitter flavor

Fizz: long, mixed drink, based on spirits and made fizzy with club soda

Flip: spirit based, creamy mixed drink made with egg

Fruit brandy: strictly speaking, brandy is distilled from fermented grapes, but many fruit brandies are distilled from whatever the fruit type is, such as apple and apricot—plum brandy, also known as slivovitz, is usually made from Mirabelle and Switzen plums

Galliano: Italian liqueur, flavored with honey and vanilla

Genever: also known as Hollands and Dutch gin, the original gin, which is sweeter and fuller-flavored than London, Plymouth, or dry gin—rarely used in cocktails (see Gin)

Gin: a colorless, grain-based spirit, strongly flavored with juniper and other herbs. London, Plymouth, and dry gin are most commonly used for cocktails

Gomme syrup: sweet syrup from France

Grand Marnier: French, orange-flavored, Cognac-based liqueur

Grappa: fiery, Italian spirit distilled from wine must

Grenadine: nonalcoholic, pomegranate-flavored syrup—used for sweetening and coloring cocktails

Irish whiskey: unblended spirit made from malted or unmalted barley and some other grains—suitable for many cocktails

Julep: originally a sweet syrup, now a family of spirit-based cocktails, flavored and decorated with fresh mint

Kahlúa: popular Mexican brand of coffee liqueur

Kirsch: colorless cherry-flavored eau-de-vie, mainly from France and Switzerland

Kümmel: colorless Dutch liqueur, flavored with caraway

Lillet: French herb-flavored liqueur, based on wine and Armagnac

Liqueur: distilled spirit flavored with such things as fruit, herbs, coffee, nuts, mint, and chocolate

London gin: the driest gin (see Gin)

Madeira: fortified wine from the island of the same name

Malibu: leading brand of coconut liqueur—based on rum

Mandarine Napoléon: Belgian, brandy-based liqueur flavored with tangerines

Maraschino: Italian, cherry-flavored liqueur—usually colorless, but may be red

Martini: popular Italian brand of vermouth produced by Martini and Rossi and also the name of a classic cocktail

Melon liqueur: spirit-based, melon-flavored liqueur—Midori is the leading brand

Midori: Japanese liqueur (see Melon liqueur)

Noilly Prat: leading French brand of very dry vermouth

Orgeat: almond-flavored syrup

Pastis: anise-flavored liqueur from France

Plymouth gin: a less dry type of gin than London gin (see Gin)

Port: Portuguese fortified wine that may be white, ruby, or tawny—white and inexpensive ruby are most appropriate for cocktails

Pousse Café: a drink poured in layers to float on top of one another, which gives its name to a narrow, straight-sided stemmed glass

Quinquina: French, wine-based apéritif, flavored with quinine

Rickey: a spirit-based cocktail including lemon or lime juice and club soda

Rum: spirit distilled from fermented sugar cane juice or molasses—light, golden, and dark have distinctive flavors and all are widely used, together and severally, in cocktails and punches

Rye whiskey: mainly American and Canadian whiskey, which must be made from a mash containing at least 51 percent rye

Sake: Japanese rice wine

Sambuca: Italian, licorice-flavored liqueur

Schnapps: grain-based spirit—available in a range of flavors, including peach and peppermint

Scotch whisky: blends are a mixture of about 40 percent malt and 60 percent grain whisky and are most suitable for cocktails—single malts should be drunk neat or diluted with water

Slammer: a cocktail mixed by slamming it on the bar

Slivovitz: plum brandy (see Fruit brandy)

Sloe gin: Liqueur made by steeping sloes in gin—previously homemade but now available commercially

Sour: a spirit-based cocktail containing sugar, and lemon or lime juice

Southern Comfort: American whiskey-based, peach-flavored liqueur

Strega: Italian, herb-flavored liqueur

Sugar syrup: a sweetener for cocktails, made by dissolving sugar in boiling water (see page 11)

Swedish Punsch: aromatic rum-based drink, flavored with wines and syrups

Tequila: Mexican spirit distilled from pulque from fermented maguey cacti

Tia Maria: popular, Jamaican rum-based coffee liqueur

Triple sec: colorless, orange-flavored liqueur

Vermouth: wine-based apéritif flavored with extracts of wormwood—both sweet and dry vermouths are widely used in cocktails

Vodka: colorless, grain-based spirit, originally from Russia and Poland. Flavored vodkas, such as lemon, raspberry, and chili, are becoming increasingly popular

Whiskey: spirit distilled from grain or malted barley—the main types are bourbon, rye, Irish, and Scotch

Cocktail List

- Absinthe Friend *100* • Acapulco *68* • Adam's Apple *118* • Alexander *46*

- American Rose *28* • Angel's Delight *196* • B and B *20* • Banshee *194*

- Between the Sheets *26* • Bishop *160* • Black Russian *88* • Bloody January *220*

- Bloody Mary *86* • Boilermaker *38* • Bosom Caresser *116* • Brave Bull *84*

- Breakfast *142* • Bronx *42* • Buck's Fizz *112* • California Smoothie *238*

- Caribbean Champagne *212* • Carolina *174* • Carrot Cream *222* • Cat's Eye *138*

- Chili Willy *176* • Cinderella *152* • Clam Digger *224* • Classic Cocktail *14*

- Club *54* • Coco Loco *166* • Corpse Reviver *22* • Cowboy *136* •

Cranberry Punch *244* • Crocodile *178* • Cuba Libre *74* • Daiquiri *70* • Daisy *50* •

Dubarry *62* • El Diablo *162* • Eye of the Hurricane *228* • Faux Kir *226*

- FBR *122* • Freedom Fighter *192* • French 75 *110* • Frozen Daiquiri *150*

- Full Monty *200* • Fuzzy Navel *184* • Godfather *190* • Grapefruit Cooler *242*

- Grasshopper *96* • Grimace and Grin *180* • Hayden's Milk Float *158*

- Highland Fling *130* • Honeymoon *126* • Huatusco Whammer *164*

- Irish Shillelagh *134* • Island Cooler *232* • Italian Soda *240* • Jade *210*

- John Wood *206* • Josiah's Bay Float *154* • Juicy Julep *230* • Kir *106*

- Lip Smacker *218* • Little Prince *234* • Long Island Iced Tea *60* • Mad Dog *204*

- Mai Tai *78* • Maiden's Blush *64* • Manhattan *34* • Margarita *80* • Martini *40*

- Melon Medley *252* • Millennium Cocktail *214* • Mint Julep *30* • Mocha Slush *246*

- Moonraker *120* • Moscow Mule *90* • Mudslide *188* • Negroni *102* • Nirvana *148*

- Old Fashioned *36* • Orange Blossom *52* • Palm Beach *156* • Panda *124*

- Piña Colada *66* • Pink Squirrel *198* • Planter's Punch *72* • Polynesian Pepper Pot *182*

- Princess *128* • Rhett Butler *98* • Rickey *56* • Road Runner *140* • Rolls Royce *104*

- Salty Dog *94* • Sangaree *16* • Screwdriver *92* • Sherry Cobbler *108*

- Shirley Temple *248* • Sidecar *18* • Singapore Sling *58* • Soft Sangria *250*

- Sparkling Peach Melba *236* • Star Bangled Spanner *202* • Stinger *24*

- Suffering Bastard *144* • Tequila Mockingbird *168* • Tequila Slammer *170*

- Tequila Sunrise *82* • Tom Collins *48* • Twin Peaks *132* • Vodga *186*

- What the Hell *146* • Which Way *208* • Whiskey Sour *32* • White Lady *44*

- Wild Night Out *172* • Zombie *76*